HEART NOTE

A CHRISTMAS ROMCOM NOVELLA

CASSANDRA O'LEARY

Heart Note: A Christmas Romcom Novella

First published in 2017

Copyright © 2017, Cassandra O'Leary

2017 eBook 1st edition, ISBN 978-1-3864304-4-5

2021 Paperback 1st edition (this edition), ISBN 978-0-6484227-0-9

Cover design by Lana Pecherczyk

Edited by Ruth Kennedy

Printed by Ingram Spark, Australia

Published by Cassandra O'Leary Author

Melbourne, Australia

cassandraolearyauthor.com

TWO WEEKS AGO...

"I can't do it." I blinked and eyed the crowd seated before me. There was no need for me to be up here on a platform in front of them. All their eyes on me.

I don't want to do it. Please don't make me.

They were all staring at me. I ran my sweaty hands down my skirt, sneaky style. But I didn't want to draw attention to my hips. I hugged myself around the waist.

"Of course you can do it. Do I have a volunteer?" The mean-eyed corporate trainer with the beaky nose and badly fitting navy suit shrugged and let out a shrill laugh. "Trust. It's crucial in a team environment." She scanned the crowd looking for willing victims. No such luck.

Beaky woman piped up again. "If I don't have a volunteer, Lily here will fail the assessment. She won't be able to start her new job."

"I don't mind, really. I'll do something else." Anything else. A new job even. No worries…

"Come on, people. I'm sure someone can catch her. She's not *that* fat." The horrible woman cackled.

Oh. My. God.

Boiling hot shame roiled through my belly and I bit my lip, hoping to slide right through the floor and into a parallel universe.

And then it happened. Just like something out of a movie. He stood up in the middle of the rows of seats, all the new staff around him staring with expressions ranging from mild interest to obvious relief.

I was nervous enough already, now he had to volunteer to help me like some sort of overly handsome dark knight to my damsel in distress. I was no damsel, but in distress? Check!

He moved into the aisle and began a slow, silent march to the front of the room where I stood.

If I fell, would he catch me?

Would I want him to let go?

Would I be too heavy and crash straight through his arms and onto the floor like a baby elephant?

Questions raced through my mind as I stood tall and concentrated hard on a square air-vent on the far wall, with two evenly spaced steel bolts and a long line underneath. If I squinted, it almost looked like a smiley face. But I didn't want to look all squinty. What if he took one look at my squinty face and sat down again?

I glanced at him quickly, so as not to look like I was

looking. But I was. He'd made his way almost to the front of the room.

Oh no. He was coming this way. What was his name? I couldn't remember. We'd all introduced ourselves briefly in a horrible 'getting to know you' game a few days ago, but it was a blur.

He was so good-looking my tongue had gone all thick and rubbery. I couldn't remember my own name. But his was Chris...something.

Christos! That's right.

I stood on the podium in front of a room full of fresh-faced new retail staff, half perky and excited, half bored out of their gourds, staring at me as if I was a museum exhibit. Only Christos volunteered to help me. He volunteered to *catch* me. He sauntered towards my spot at the front of the room. My knees quaked. For real.

Christos. A gorgeous Greek-god-like name for a gorgeous Greek-god-like man. Or a fallen angel, some sort of demigod. Or part demon maybe. I shook my head, the fanciful ideas getting in the way of the important work of real-life ogling. Today he was wearing a fine black wool sweater and dark denim jeans, which hugged some truly impressive thighs. I don't know when I'd ever been impressed by a man's thighs before, but I was now. Mightily.

And I was staring with intent. I wouldn't have had to spell out my intent, if it came to the point. I'm sure my goo-goo eyes conveyed the message, loud and clear.

I remembered now, he would be a security officer at the same store where I was going to work. I snapped my eyes upwards before he arrested me for most likely illegal thoughts about a colleague... Not helping my distractedness. I could have dealt with Christos snapping handcuffs on my wrists.

Yes, sir.

He sauntered some more, coming right up to the baby-poo-brown carpet square in front of the podium, and me. Only about thirty centimetres separated us, but honestly it felt like less. A beat of my heart, no more.

"Hi." He said the short word with a depth of feeling and throatiness, leaving me temporarily speechless. His eyes were so dark. Penetrating. "Are you all right?"

I nodded, furiously, so as not to give the wrong idea. The wrong idea being that I didn't want him to catch me.

The trainer, who I'd momentarily forgotten even existed, cleared her throat. "Right! Are we ready? As I was saying, trust is super important between team members. This exercise is a great bonding activity!"

I don't know why the woman was so excited about corporate training, but she was just so damned perky, or evil, I wasn't sure which. I didn't know whether to laugh or vomit. I settled for swallowing hard, ignoring the dry-throat syndrome Christos induced.

He raised one eyebrow and quirked the corner of

his mouth, sending me into a head spin I didn't quite recover from before he spoke. "Turn around."

Whoosh! My underwear went up in flames.

Okay, not quite, but I was worried the smoke alarm on the ceiling would go off. I did enjoy being bossed around by the right man.

I turned on the podium so my back was to him. Suddenly, my spidey sense tingled. Or maybe it was my pheromones sparking with his. He was so close behind me I could feel his body heat emanating towards me, massaging the back of my neck. Or it could have been his fingers. Oh! It was his fingers.

And his scent...honeyed cinnamon and lemongrass wrapped around my olfactory gland and made it very happy indeed. A good-looking and a good-smelling man—a rare and delicious combination.

With a tap on my shoulder, he rumbled, "I'm right behind you." His hands were gone. A whoosh of cool air followed.

This was it.

Crunch time.

I had to trust Christos.

I had to fall.

I closed my eyes, scrunching my eyelids tight so not even a sliver of light got past them. I let my head tip back. My body dropped low and lax, my knees bent, my heart pounded in my ears. And I pushed off.

I fell.

Into his arms.

His strong, reliable arms were wrapped around my waist. His chest was pressed to my back and oh, yes. He had me. But I was possibly having a heart attack.

"My heart," I said, and he smiled. Perfectly straight white teeth flashed at me, while some kind of rampantly handsome smile lines danced on his face.

Dazzling. Dazzled. Dazed?

Whatever the proper word for what I was feeling, I was in a kerfuffle. Understatement of the millennium.

"I'm here," he mumbled, only for my ears. "Trust me."

Oh, hubba hubba.

Something warm and lovely swelled under my breasts. Maybe this job wouldn't be so bad after all.

CHAPTER 1

❄

"**E**xperience the rush of pure Christmas pleasure...
Heart-mas." *Heart-mas, Heart-mas, Heart-mas...*

The words echoed, and were followed up by a
thumpity, thump sound to mimic a heartbeat, then a
screeching violin note to finish. The stupid ad played
over and over again on the flat-screen TV monitor
directly overhanging Harrison's department store
perfume counter.

The same ad was playing on a whole wall of TV
screens beside the escalators and the central gold-
bauble-bedecked Christmas tree near where I stood. I
was ready, perfume spritzer in hand, to spray any
unsuspecting customers who came my way. I had now
heard the ad approximately eleventy billion times since
I started work here two weeks ago, and I tell you,
familiarity breeds contempt.

The video matched the voice-over in being annoying. It featured a wraith-like poppet of a supermodel in a low-cut, bright-red jumpsuit and reindeer antlers dancing in slow motion. She still managed to look fabulous.

It wasn't fair. If I wore the same outfit I'd look like an overgrown preschooler in a Christmas play with a slight weight problem. Not that I was fat, I was simply naturally endowed with 'womanly curves and child-bearing hips', as my gran used to say. *Urgh.*

The Heart-mas scent was the big promotional drawcard of the season and we had been instructed to promote the hell out of it, whether we liked it or not. I did not. The top note of the perfume was suffused with something I can only describe as skanky old socks, while the middle note, or Heart Note, reminded me of blue cheese.

I hadn't been able to stand the scent on my skin for long enough to discover whatever the delightful base note could be. It didn't improve on closer acquaintance. I spent a good ten minutes in the staff bathroom yesterday, scrubbing the offending odour from my wrist.

I glanced across the cosmetics floor and my gaze was hooked on a vision of beauty. The Greek-Australian security guard, Christos. Causer of fake heart attacks and truly exceptional partner in trust exercises demanded by staff trainers.

Hello! I squinted at him across the floor. I'd love to make his closer acquaintance. I sighed as he turned and strode off, talking on his walkie-talkie the whole time and looking important. His furrowed brow made him look both angry and sexy. Sexy-angry?

Hello, Mr Sangry. At least he had something to do apart from make up new words.

The day had started like any other day on the department store cosmetics floor, which was to say, slow as a wet week. It was only the start of November, but apparently it was Christmas time in retail land. Shoppers hadn't quite caught on yet.

So, at nine o'clock opening time, the polished marble tile floors echoed with the lonely clicks of spritzer-chick heels, as we roamed the department with perfume bottles and cards printed with images of roses or the curling script of the perfume's name. Chicks like me, working their way through university or saving their pennies, one fragrant spritz at a time.

My brand new black pencil skirt and slightly puffy white blouse were starchy and scratchy, but my make-up was expertly applied, eyebrows appropriately arched and unruly auburn curls tamed (for now) into swishy submission in a low ponytail tied with a black satin bow. Dare I say, the outfit actually looked good on me. It was a 1940s look, flattering my hips rather than accentuating any lumps and bumps. Paired with my Mary Jane heels, I thought it worked.

I gave up on spritzing non-existent customers for now, and strolled back towards what I dubbed Perfume HQ. The square arrangement of glass and chrome counters surrounding a central column, cash register and wrapping area was a scent-lovers' paradise. Hundreds of different perfumes were here from Paris, London, New York and around the world. All packaged in shiny boxes and glittering glass bottles. I loved it. I would have loved it more if it had been my own perfumery. One day, hopefully. It was my long-term goal.

I craned my neck around the towering display of fragrance gift sets I had so carefully arranged yesterday. Perfectly wrapped and be-ribboned, resplendent in their Christmassy gold paper and red-velvet bows. The pyramid-shaped display on the low table in the aisle seemed precarious to me, but what did I know? I knew perfume, but I wasn't the visual merchandising expert. She'd suggested it, so I'd gone along with the idea.

Speak of the devil...

Lynda 'with a Y' McCauley, Visual Merchandising Manager, was out and about. I noted heads ducking behind nearby make-up counters, staff pretending to rearrange stock in low cabinets. Hiding, basically.

Lynda was not a woman to be crossed. She'd have you re-wrapping hundreds of already beautifully wrapped gift sets before you could say 'management track control freak'.

"Good morning, Petal. How are we today?"

I narrowed my eyes an infinitesimal amount. I hated when Lynda called me *Petal*. Hated it with the loathing usually reserved for stinky-cheese perfume. My name was Lily Lucas, as she was well aware. The name tag pinned to my blouse stated my first name anyway. I blinked slowly and allowed a polite but non-committal smile to cross my dial. Maybe Lynda was being funny, trying to be my friend. I was the new girl, after all.

Tilting my chin in her direction, I tried to strike up a conversation. "I'm fine, thanks. Just getting started on the new displays." I waved my arm vaguely at the stack of newly arrived perfumes and body creams lying on the wrapping table behind me.

Unfortunately, the gentle waving action of my arm sent a breeze rippling towards the pyramid-shaped stack of boxes, which were not, in fact, actual presents but pretend packages. They were quite hollow. Lightweight.

They toppled and fell like a stack of dominoes, clunking on the table and down around my feet. I kept my eyes up, pressing my lips together to keep from laughing, or crying. As a final death knell, the Perspex sign behind the display fell down with a low *wallop*.

I met Lynda's accusatory eyes, steely grey and mean with it. She glanced down at the floor and muttered something under her breath, which may have been something derogatory about lazy retail workers. I crossed my arms over my stomach.

Lynda looked up and leaned right over the counter, her claw-like hands gripping the chrome edge. Her jet black bob swung over the super-wide shoulder pads of her 1980s-style Chanel power suit. She partly bared her teeth in what may have been a smile. "I'm glad you said you're just getting started, because the display wasn't much good, was it? Piss. Weak. Do it again."

My stomach dropped and the delicious latte I'd downed on the walk to work turned sour and squelchy in my gut. Lynda was evidently in a mood, again. But I bit my tongue to stop myself swearing and surveyed the mess.

Out of the corner of my eye I saw Lynda turn and march off, clacking across the floor on her stunningly high Louboutins, towards the other new girls at the manicure bar.

One of them, Petula, I'd met in training. She was a qualified hairdresser/make-up artist who looked like a Bollywood movie star. Petula caught my eye and raised her eyebrows in alarm. Petula...*Petal*... I think Lynda had me confused with the other new hire across the floor. At least I'd give Lynda the benefit of the doubt and assume so.

With a sigh, I turned to the scattered boxes, plus the other pile of products to be arranged. My Thursday offsider, the reliable Gillian, would be in at ten, so she could help. But since I was the counter manager, I'd have to come up with the overall plan.

The direction from Lynda had been vague, to say the least. "*Festive. But not hideous with gold baubles everywhere.*" Right.

I lifted my head to examine the ceiling decorations and couldn't help but notice the sheer volume of gold baubles dangling overhead from garlands of pretend pine leaves. They threatened to fall and poke my eyes out any second.

With my eyes trained above, I didn't notice I'd stepped on a slippery satin ribbon, which skated across the floor, taking me with it.

Woah!

I let out a gasp and then an unladylike cry of pain as the hard floor met both my arse and the back of my head. Pleased to meet you, *clunk*. Likewise, *crack*!

I stared up at the baubles and the lights above, blinking stupidly. I should get up. Really, I should. Only I suddenly wanted to curl into a ball right there and have a little nap.

I sat up part-way, leaning on my elbows. I grabbed a handful of perfume spritz cards that were by my side.

"Problem?"

The gruff and quite frankly lady-parts-spasm-inducing voice of senior security guard and all-round hottie, Christos, caused me to drop the pile of spritzer cards. They fell to the floor like a randomly shuffled deck of cards. I was feeling pretty randomly shuffled too, when I glanced up and met his eyes.

He was all stunning in a Zeus-like way, clad in a perfectly fitted grey suit and white shirt (courtesy of the men's fashion department on the fourth floor). His brown eyes reminded me of half-melty chocolate buttons. Of course he had the type of thick, velvety looking hair I itched to run my hands through. I stared. I couldn't help it.

"Baubles," I babbled.

"Excuse me?" Christos arched one dark, manly eyebrow. It really was manly. He had a thoughtful expression on his face too, like the famous sculpture, The Thinker. You know, the naked, muscular one? Anyway, Christos had his Thinker face on and I paused to admire him. He tilted his head to one side and waited me out.

Then he reached over and extended an excessively masculine hand in my direction. I grabbed hold and warmth wrapped around me. I let him help me to my feet because I couldn't manage in my tight skirt. I didn't mind the excuse to touch him, either. I stumbled, grabbing hard onto his forearm before I righted myself and leaned back against the counter.

Christos tilted his head again, his gaze travelling thoughtfully up and down my body. At least I thought it was in regards to my body. Maybe he was busy thinking about what he wanted for lunch.

"What happened?" he asked with a quasi-smile, only there for a moment.

"It was just Lynda being a pain in my arse. I spent hours on my displays already but then this lot fell over in front of her. Apparently I'm no good at decorating and I have to start again. Without too many baubles." I sighed, gesturing vaguely with my right hand to the threatening baubles overhead.

"Right." He nodded, then leaned in, over the counter, whispering right near my ear. "She's a pain in my arse too. Wants me to count and catalogue all the mannequin hands in the back storage room. She's convinced someone is stealing them. I tried to tell her it's not my job but…" He shook his head and then rolled his eyes skyward.

I pressed my lips together to stifle a laugh and glanced over his shoulder in the direction of women's fashion. Lynda was now patrolling like a police officer, skirting the perimeter and narrowing her eyes at a pedestal featuring two mannequins in red sequined party dresses. They appeared to have their hands in place.

When I returned my gaze to Christos's handsome face, he quickly met my eyes. "I like red lipstick on you. Much better than the vampire purple from last week." He hesitated, his mouth opening as if to say something else. "Have a good day."

He stepped back from my counter and strode away towards the security station near the store's entrance doors. I was left gaping after him.

Christos had noticed my lipstick. My *lips*. Maybe I should have been insulted that he'd commented, but I wasn't. I was warm and tingly.

Maybe it would be a good day after all. My hand was still warm from where I'd grasped his hand, then his arm. He was strong. Not just normal-man strong, but muscular. I knew he was, because I'd felt his forearm flex under my fingertips. It was like steel.

Then I clocked Petula giving me raised eyebrows from across the floor. Her gaze followed the path Christos had taken.

Petula winked, and her golden-tinted eyelids twinkled. I'd have to ask her about the eyeshadow she was wearing. It was super glam. Petula mimed a coffee drinking action and pointed to her chest, then to me.

I nodded, glancing towards the front doors of the store. Sure, morning coffee break together at 10.30 am. It was a date.

Petula would want all the Christos-related gossip. There wasn't much to tell, so I'd have to get my embellishments ready. There was no need to ruin a perfectly good flirtation story with too much pesky reality, after all.

I spotted Petula right away at Georgina's, the best Italian café in the still half-empty mall. She sat neatly with her legs crossed to one side, unaware she was showing off her sheer black stockings and towering high heels in her little black uniform dress, which was quite chic. *Va-va-voom!*

She was also apparently unaware of the avid male attention she was currently receiving from the barista, the delivery boy, who nearly dropped a box full of coffee beans on his foot, and one or two of the customers near the counter who had their mouths hanging open.

Petula's table was beside the wall of windows overlooking the ocean of cars in the car park of the southern hemisphere's largest indoor shopping centre. Not exactly a delightful view, but there were a few potted plants out the front.

My new friend waved me over to her table, grinning like a gossip-crazed maniac. Which she undoubtedly was, but in an endearing way, like a puppy eager for treats. Petula wasted no time in picking my brain for tantalising titbits of gossip. At the last minute I decided against confiding in her about how much I liked Christos. It seemed too soon.

Petula leaned forward, her eyes wide. "Did he ask you out, or did he tell you he thinks you're beautiful while creasing his forehead and running his fingers across his stubble? Because I had a dream like that."

I shook my head. "Um, no."

Petula's face fell for a moment, but then she sat to attention and her eyes widened further. "Or did he slowly unbutton his shirt and let you smell his neck? Because I have to say, he stood close behind me last Wednesday in the lunch queue at Romani's and he smells divine."

"Look, I hate to disappoint you, but we really only talked about baubles."

"Baubles?"

"The Christmas decorations. I can't believe I have to do my displays again. He didn't laugh, which would have been fair enough. Christos empathised with me about Lynda. She's giving him a hard time too."

Petula grinned. "Oh, good. You've got something in common!"

I let out a laugh under my breath. Petula was determined to set me up with someone. That she'd happened to pick on the very man I'd been crushing on since I'd fallen into his arms at staff training either meant she could read my mind and we were bound to be best friends forever, or she fancied him as much as I did. But I happened to know she had her eye on someone else.

I tipped my head to one side and asked her, casual as you please, "So when are you seeing Kurt again?" The shy Kurt was her study partner from her accounting class.

Petula blushed, a dead-set, deep vermillion, even under her caramel skin tone. It would make a fabulous shade of lipstick. "There must be a story to go along with your blush."

With a shrug, Petula brushed her long, silky ponytail over one shoulder. "He's taking me out Friday night. Bowling! Can you believe it? I don't know how I'll manage with these nails." She glanced at her perfectly manicured hands, now featuring the latest season's nail colour, turquoise metallic, with decals of little golden stars and moons.

I reached out and stroked one of her nails. "Amazing. But not for bowling."

"Right? Anyhoo, I checked out bowling shoes online and they totally have purple glittery ones I could buy."

A grin stretched out my cheeks until they could have burst like mini balloons. "Sounds like a serious relationship, if it requires special shoes."

She bit her lip, hesitating, but she was smiling. "Maybe."

I was happy for her. Petula's skin actually radiated happiness, and I didn't think it was the result of the primer she'd tried from the organic skincare counter. No, she was radiant because she'd found a man who wanted to hang out and take her *bowling*. It wasn't even a euphemism for anything dirty.

We chatted for a few minutes as we drank coffee. Petula told me all about the oddball professor teaching her accounting classes. I told her all about my stoush with my new next-door neighbour. We were arguing about when to bring in the rubbish bins on a Friday.

Then Petula's expression turned all serious. Her lips formed a thin line. "Can I ask you something? When you worked at the perfumery in Sydney, did you like being able to come and go as you pleased? I mean, you were the boss of the shop."

I paused to say thanks to the new young waiter for bringing over another coffee. He was only about seventeen, doing his final exams in high school. About the same age as my little sister.

He looked down at me under long blonde lashes, then murmured something like, "My pleasure, babe." I shot him a frown of disapproval but he was already headed back to the serving area behind the cake display.

Petula watched me stir a teaspoon of raw sugar into my latte, dissolving the fine golden crystals into the leaf pattern the barista, Yusef, had made in the top of the milk foam. He really was an artist. I shot him a genuine smile across the cafe, and he grinned before ducking his head behind the coffee machine again.

Now *he* seemed like a sweetheart who I would seriously consider dating, if he wasn't already going out with the pretty but perpetually harassed Belinda, the pastry chef.

I sighed as I swallowed a mouthful of the excellent coffee, letting it warm me through to my bones and send wake-up messages to all my nerve endings. Then I met my friend's eyes and answered her question, as honestly as possible.

"I loved my job. I never would have left if I didn't have to."

I'd had a hard time in the few months since I was forced to leave my previous job at a stand-alone, boutique perfumery in inner-city Sydney. I couldn't find another job with the same level of responsibility or salary there, so I ended up moving to Melbourne where rent was cheaper, although not by much. My little place in fashionable Malvern would cost a significant chunk of change.

The department store job wasn't my first choice, but at least I was still in the perfume trade. I had experience from working in a similar store a few years ago. And I could walk to and from work, saving both travel costs and gym fees. This should be a good move. But I still sighed when I thought of the old perfumery, which had felt like home.

I gazed into space over Petula's shoulder, picturing the shop as it had been. "I loved the perfumery. The old-fashioned stained-glass windows, the hand-crafted cabinets, the French blown-glass bottles, all of it. Just walking in the door and inhaling the profusion of perfumes made me happy."

The shop had been there for over a hundred years. I'd worked my way up to be weekday manager, but I wasn't the boss. "Judith was the boss, and like family. Her stamp was all over the place, from the inventory we purchased from France, to the design of the brochures we sent out to customers. Until she was gone. I miss her."

Judith, the octogenarian owner, had been my perfumier mentor. She'd died about four months ago, leaving the shop to her middle-aged son. He promptly fired the staff and sold the shop, liquidating the assets. The heartless fiend spent it all on a luxury boat to sail around Sydney Harbour, or so I'd heard.

Petula's mouth twisted to one side. "I'm sorry about

Judith and the shop. But you're on the right track with this job. Being counter manager at a big department store is a great thing to have on your CV."

I nodded, then glanced out the window. A pigeon chose to leave his business on the pane of glass. I sighed. "I know, so everyone keeps telling me. It's hard when I'm still studying part-time. At least the term is over for summer. Then I'll do online classes. But I didn't want to leave my sister." Not to put too fine a point on it, but I was broke and I'd had no choice but to take this job.

Petula's voice went soft and wistful, and she waved her hands around in mid-air. "One day, it will all be worth it. You'll have your marketing degree and your own shop. You'll be the bossest perfume boss ever. You'll have beautiful perfumes shipped from France and design your own bottles. And you can hire me to be your make-up artist on staff. Life will be perfect."

The vision was tantalising, a golden-haloed, richly scented image in my imagination. Unfortunately it was still out of reach by several years and many thousands of dollars. Still, Petula was proving to be a good friend, trying to make me think positive.

"Thanks, honey."

"You're welcome. Now, tell me about how you're going to implement some extreme flirting strategies with Christos while you're working here."

A gurgly laugh escaped my throat, as I'd been sipping my glass of water. Petula was studying a business degree and loved talking about implementing strategies and being 'agile'. She also loved spreadsheets, but I wouldn't hold it against her as an otherwise normal person.

Suddenly, the peace of the café was shattered by a violent, ear-splitting alarm, then the rush of people. Two, no three, guys in black hoodies and jeans ran past the café doors and out through the main mall entrance. They made it out to the car park, still running, ducking and weaving around a bus and a line of taxis.

Then I saw him. A vision of athletic perfection, an Olympian in a business shirt and trousers. Christos was sprinting after them. I hardly had a second to admire him as he shot out of sight. The police pulled up outside the main entrance in a divvy van. They'd arrived quickly. They wouldn't send a van unless a crime was unfolding.

Petula and I glanced at each other and shrugged, then stared out the window, trying to make out any activity. What was going on?

Perhaps today wasn't simply a day like any other. How exciting! I couldn't wait to find out the full story. I'd have to corner Christos later.

Hmmm, cornering Christos. The idea had possibilities.

CHAPTER 2

I arrived at work early the next day, clocking in at eight o'clock, only to find myself barred from entering the cosmetics floor. The main way in from the staff area was cordoned off with yellow and black tape. Christos and a couple of his team were there, sexily directing everyone to stay out of the way.

Christos was sexy anyway, with his bossy face on, wearing a black suit and grey shirt underneath. He stood with his arms crossed, legs shoulder width apart, talking on his walkie-talkie.

Had there been an accident or some other incident related to whatever happened yesterday? I couldn't work out the cause of the situation. Of course I had to ask.

I sidled up to him. "Christos, what's going on? It's okay, you can tell me." I fluttered my eyelashes at him, shamelessly.

He didn't quite crack a smile, but his eyes wrinkled up at the corners in the most adorable way. "It's the new visual merchandising display for the central aisle. They need a scissor lift to get it up on the pedestal."

I cocked my head to the right and looked past Christos to the gigantic glass object currently being hoisted up above head height on a mechanical doohickey I could only assume was a 'scissor lift'. It had foldy metal parts under a platform, unfurling now, concertina style. The platform rose higher. I spotted one of the maintenance crew sitting in a small cabin below, operating it like a forklift driver.

Someone stood on the platform. Lynda. She had one hand on top of the object, steadying whatever the glass thing was. A couple of black-clad team members were now on the floor below, directing traffic. They told the driver to inch forward, now right, a little left, aiming for the top of a towering white pedestal in the centre aisle.

I watched, half mesmerised, half terrified the thing would crash down on someone's head. Although if it crashed on Lynda, maybe it wouldn't be the end of the world.

Christos called out in his gruff, commanding voice. "Stand back."

I took a step back as instructed, towards him. A couple of other floor staff had arrived to watch and the security team ushered them well behind the tape.

Another great piece of machinery came into view. A

crane arm was attached to the lift, extending upwards, hooking onto the top of the display piece. It was half covered in bubble wrap.

Finally, the object was placed on top of the pedestal and Lynda carefully removed the bubble wrap. The overhead lights hit the facades of the largest crystal perfume bottle I'd ever seen. It was an oversized replica of the Heart-mas bottle. Almost as large as a person.

I gasped. "It's beautiful."

"Yes, it's beautiful. And expensive. Requires an extra security detail." Christos spoke in a low voice, rumbling from just behind my right shoulder.

I glanced over my shoulder to meet his eyes. He had his intense stare going on again. It was almost as if he was interrogating me with his gaze, or stripping me naked. I shivered, and my attention dropped to his mouth. I pressed my own lips together, preparing to say something, anything. Ask him out on a date, maybe?

But the screech of high heels behind me made me whip around on the spot. It was Petula. She grabbed my arm and pulled me towards the perfume counter, shouting over her shoulder, "Hi, Christos. Nice day for looking so handsome!"

I laughed. I'd been a bit down earlier, worrying over money and about my sister, who was staying with friends in Sydney. She was fine, or so I'd heard. Mrs Martin, Deidre, treated KC like a second daughter, so I trusted her word. But my stubborn sister wouldn't return my phone calls.

But I wouldn't mope. Today was a day for admiring beauty and enjoying future possibilities. Because I said so. I enjoyed watching Christos during the day while I worked, as he moved across a crowded cosmetics floor, weaving fluidly, like a ninja, through throngs of shoppers.

"Oh. My. God." My reaction couldn't be contained, unfortunately.

Had I forgotten to drink my second cup of coffee? Because I was clearly delusional. The vision before me had to be caffeine-deficiency induced.

I'd had some time to wind down from the events of the day before, with no explanation as to what was going on from either Christos or the store management. I expected we'd find out eventually if there had been a crime going down. But today's excitement was of a different variety.

When I saw the new casual staff walking towards my counter, my mouth popped open. I leaned forward on the perfume counter, mouth agape like a stunned mullet. It was probably unprofessional, but I couldn't help it.

I turned to Giselle, standing at my right.

Giselle was a willowy French import with a hypnotic accent, naturally highlighted brunette hair and friendly personality that put anyone at ease. To her left stood Gillian, the non-exotic but reliable and hardworking country girl, with silky blonde hair, freckles and perfect teeth. Collectively, they were known as G-G or Gigi. According to me.

"Gigi, what do you make of this?"

Gillian was near the towering display of perfume tester bottles arranged on a precarious kind of multi-level, mirrored Lazy Susan. She shook her head. "No."

Giselle shrugged, her long and lush false lashes fluttered as she blinked several times.

The new gang of casual spritzer chicks walked in close formation, either in solidarity or trying to hide somehow. Because the costumes they sported were truly horrendous. A crime against fashion, not to mention reindeers. And Christmas.

Red onesies. Gold reindeer antlers. Oh, no...

"White boots! What were they thinking?" Giselle had read my mind. She continued to *tsk* under her breath, clearly appalled.

The new girls looked like a sleigh full of Rudolph and Mrs Claus costumes had exploded after a run-in with a bad 80s music video. Their hair wasn't teased on end, but was slicked back to allow the gold sparkly antlers maximum wow-factor. It was the Heart-mas perfume ad come to life in front of me, in scary 3D with added velour and 'smell-a-vision'. The aroma was truly something. An eye-watering something no perfume lover should ever suffer.

Giselle sighed with gusto and tapped me on the shoulder. "Please, tell me *we* will not have to wear *that*?"

It hadn't occurred to me. I shuddered, because why wouldn't I? "I don't think so. No one has mentioned a costume to me. It's not in the product-knowledge brochure or the communiques from head office." I waved vaguely at the folders of information and promotional material filed under the cash register.

The posse of new girls reached the counter in front of me, all of them sharing dazed and confused expressions. The one at the front of the pack, bearing the name 'Penny' on her name tag, looked close to tears.

I pulled myself up to full height, five foot five in heels, and forced myself into calm, professional mode. I'd been expecting new staff, if not their mad two-dollar-shop costume-party appearance. "Welcome everyone. I'm Lily, the counter manager. Your fearless leader." I saluted, for fun.

A few of the women smiled and said hello. I did a quick head count. Eight casual staff had arrived. Quite a large crew, and more than I'd been expecting. I'd put them to work though. I'd booked a training room and would have them gift wrapping before I unleashed them on the cosmetics floor for promotions.

After a quick pep talk, and they needed the pep, I ushered them away, the new girls headed towards the training room. I'd be gone for half an hour. An hour, tops. The gift wrapping in the training room would be quicker with a whole team. Still, I wanted to make sure my regular staff were okay.

Gillian was busy straightening the display in the glass-fronted cabinets, making sure the gold boxes of a swanky brand were prominently displayed.

I waved at Giselle where she was crouched behind the counter, pulling stock out of the drawers at floor level. "Bye, G. See you in a while. Oh, don't forget to fill in your sales sheet for the week."

Giselle nodded once. "Of course. Good luck with the new...girls." Her lips twisted to one side for a second. Elegant as she was, this was her contained version of a guffaw.

I raised my freshly waxed eyebrows. "Thanks for the support."

I lead the newbies across the ground floor to the training room out past women's fashion. They cooed over the new season's clothes as we went. I didn't blame them.

The Spring Racing displays were well done. They were a constant temptation to spend up on my credit card. The mannequins wore elegant retro-style dresses in a bouquet of fresh colours, and fancy hats adorned with feathers and ribbons. Rows of matching accessories including purses and necklaces were displayed on low tables. It was like a sweet shop full of treats for grown women.

I ushered the newbies away from the goodies and towards the training room at the end of a long corridor. This area was only accessible to staff, but this lot had all cleared a security check with their promotional agency to get the job.

We were near the changing rooms to the left of the warehouse-style storeroom when from the corner of my eye I saw Petula hand-signalling. She was near a rack of black jackets, hopping from foot to foot as if she had to go to the loo.

"Lily!" Petula stage-whispered at me, while ducking her head behind the rack of jackets.

I craned my neck to the right to see what she might be up to. Who knew? I told the group of casuals to go on through to the training room. They each scanned their Visitor cards as they passed through the door.

I approached Petula with caution. Had she completely lost the plot? She was crouched low to the floor now and had a twitchy look. "Are you okay?" I asked. "Do you want me to call someone?"

Petula shout-whispered again, her eyes wide. "You need to talk to Christos. Something weird is going on around here."

"You don't say? You're hiding under a rack of clothes, acting like you're on the run from the law. You're not on the run, are you?"

Petula flicked her hair over her shoulder and looked behind her. "No! At least, I don't think so. But the police *were* here asking lots of questions. Christos said they want to talk to all the new staff."

Weird. But it didn't explain Petula's current crab-like scurrying in the fashion department. "Right, I'll see if I can find Christos soon. But tell me what you're hiding from."

"Oh, it's time for volunteer sign-ups for the staff fun run. I'm hiding from Katya from Homewares. I don't run for anyone!"

This was a pretty good reason to hide, I had to admit. Walking was one thing, but running was some kind of self-induced torture. Why anyone would consider it fun was beyond me. "I think you're in the clear. See you later, okay?"

"Okay!" Petula scurried away, more crab-like than ever, moving across the floor towards her own counter.

I took off down the corridor after the red-onesie crew, my heels clicking against the polished concrete as I went. All I had to do was train them enough so they wouldn't scare the customers. I had my work cut out for me.

CHAPTER 3

A couple of hours later, Penny led the new team through the main aisle of the cosmetics floor. She was spritzing for all she was worth, full credit to her. I stayed on the perfume counter with Giselle, wrapping gifts and ringing up purchases.

The customers weren't too sure about the fragrance. I couldn't blame them. An older woman dressed in a fine wool cardigan and day dress screwed up her nose and said, "No thank you, dear." She raised her right hand and backed away.

I ducked my head to hide my smile as a new customer approached the counter. I looked up, then ratcheted my neck higher still. She may have been the tallest woman I'd seen in real life. Beautiful too, in a model-like ice-princess way. A modern Hitchcock blonde. She was all cheekbones and pouty lips, and so close I almost forgot to breathe. *Wow.*

Veronica Versuvius, model-slash-actress-slash-singer and probably a few other slashes I'd forgotten. She was here. In my store. In front of me.

Trying not to stare (but probably failing) I tried to look welcoming, not like a complete screaming fangirl about to have a meltdown. I might be a fangirl but I didn't want to seem like it. She was an incredible actress who melted into the skin of her characters. I loved her in the blockbuster with the hunky English actor, Richard Heath. When they kissed it was ultra-swoony.

Veronica tipped her chin at me and trailed an elegant hand along the edge of the glass and chrome counter. "Do you have the parfum concentrate of Elixir?"

I sighed because I loved the perfume. Forgetting who I was talking to, I gushed like a perfume fangirl. "Oh, I love this fragrance. Isn't it divine? It's so complex with lily of the valley and French lavender top notes, then honeysuckle and amber layers come through."

I stepped to the right and bent before a low cabinet, unlocking it with the key attached to my staff card. This was where the special products were kept. "I have a couple of bottles tucked away, only for our exclusive customers."

I reached for the gorgeous white satin box with an actual gold-plated lid, tiny butterfly with delicate wings lifting off from the top. The bottle was cut crystal in an old-fashioned style with an elaborate stopper, like a Lalique art glass piece. I carefully lifted the box with both hands. I must have made a gushing noise, because Veronica responded.

"I know, I love the bottle. It's a work of art."

I handed the perfume to her, taking utmost care not to drop it or fall on my face, since I'd been such an uncoordinated disaster lately.

She took it with her hand extended palm up, then wrapped her fingers around the base. "So beautiful. I'll take it!"

I gasped, not even trying to hide my reaction. This bottle was exclusive based on price alone. Over seven hundred dollars' worth of exclusivity. Veronica placed her platinum credit card in my hand and I could have squealed to see her name typed on the card, just like on the credits of a movie screen.

I rang up the purchase like the professional I was, scanning Veronica's card. Then I wrapped the perfume in the best gift box I could find—a white embossed box with a black velvet ribbon. I made sure to hide any sticky tape and cut the ends of the ribbon on a forty-five-degree angle so it looked fabulous. Then I placed it in a shopping bag.

I popped the bag on the counter. "Can I ask you a movie question? It's nothing too weird, I promise."

Veronica pressed her lips together, then offered a tight smile. "All right, shoot."

I sucked in a deep breath, then let the words tumble out. "What was it like kissing Richard Heath?"

Veronica laughed lightly, the sound like a wind chime. "It was nice. Actually, he's an exceptional kisser." She glanced over each of her shoulders, as if checking for eavesdroppers.

I spied her entourage of two black-suited security guards near the escalators, trying but failing to blend in as regular shoppers. Big, burly blokes hanging out near the anti-aging skincare counter were a dead giveaway. They crossed their arms over their broad chests and hovered there without making eye contact with anyone, which was odd.

Veronica leaned in over the counter. "I demanded re-take after re-take. I was a real diva, which isn't normally like me. It was worth it even if the director was fuming." Veronica's sapphire-blue eyes shimmered with mischief.

A burble of laughter burst from my throat. I didn't expect her to be cool. Maybe we could be best friends forever. Then my bubble burst.

Veronica said, "Thanks for your help." She walked away. Not my BFF then.

Across the floor I spotted Christos now standing with the two burly security guys. They were chatting like old mates, laughing and slapping each other on the back. I wondered if Christos knew Veronica? I filed the thought away for later.

CHAPTER 4

❄

Time passed, not always too slowly. I settled into my job and finally Christmas shoppers descended. This particular day, a red sea of casual spritzer chicks spread out across the department, from the main entrance of the store to the bottom of the escalators. They handed out mini perfume vials attached to sample cards.

Even I had to admit the costumes looked effective from a distance. The scarlet velour jumpsuits stood out like a sore thumb, but they matched the Christmassy décor in the store with the hanging pine laurels and suspended sparkly baubles. In their costumes, the girls looked like red rose petals scattered across the floor.

A pop tune came ringing out from the P.A. system. It had me humming and feeling positively festive. Mariah Carey's modern classic, *All I Want For Christmas Is You* was irresistible. I hummed along, swaying and hip-bumping with Giselle as we went about our cabinet stocking. But my good mood didn't last.

B y two-thirty, I could stand it no longer.

We'd had a flood of customers since eleven, with no let-up. I'd had no break and was rapidly becoming a ravenous beast-monster. Customers were hovering around the perfume counter like bees seeking pollen. But I had to eat and sit down before I either bit someone's head off or passed out. I leaned on the edge of the counter and took a deep breath.

I pressed a hand to my stomach as it gurgled. "I need lunch. Can you hold the fort?"

I cast the question over my shoulder at my team members, who had each just finished serving a couple of 'high-touch' customers, as they'd say in marketing class. These were customers requiring a high level of service and hand-holding, all our ad-speak, upselling and product-knowledge expertise. In other words, they were exhausting.

"Yes, though I will need a break soon too. My feet are killing me!" This, from Giselle, wasn't surprising. Her shoes were always skyscraper-high designer numbers, gorgeous but impractical.

I glanced at her feet and swallowed a stab of shoe-envy. Those beauties were worth the pain. High heels with black and white stripes on the little bows adorning the instep. Sweet but sexy too.

I nodded at the girls in turn. "Okay, Gigi, you go in half an hour and we'll crossover."

I strolled away towards the staff-only area through fitness apparel, and stiffened as I felt a presence close behind me. It wasn't unheard of to be followed by male customers. I was wary ever since a young woman from kitchenware had to enlist security to walk her to her car. Everyone was talking about it.

I glanced over my shoulder and my heart hippity-hopped with excitement to find Christos walking behind me. But he didn't look up. He was watching his own feet as he walked. Then he was right beside me. He wanted to talk to me. My tummy tightened at the thought.

He walked at my pace, and I felt his sideways glance. My heart jitterbugged like I'd been listening to Wham! on the 80s radio station I liked.

He cleared his throat. "Lily, do you have a moment?"

I fluttered my eyelashes without thinking. "For you, all the moments." Where had this flirty fox sprung from? I was usually tongue-tied when I met a man I liked. Or wanted to have babies with, whatever.

He frowned in a crinkly way. "Good to know. The break room okay?"

"Sure. Give me five minutes."

I scooted off to the staff bathroom to powder my nose. In my case, it wasn't a euphemism. I got horrible shiny skin after wearing thick make-up under the store's lights. So I primped and primed in front of the mirror, applying translucent powder from my compact, then Red Hot Mama lipstick and my favourite Better Than Sex mascara. I was perfectly prettified again. Exiting the Ladies, I veered right to the secure area where we stored our bags and personal items during our shifts.

Then I dashed into the break room and immersed myself in its awfulness. With its chipped laminate tables, and old magazines, the whole look could have been dropped in from my old living room, back when we still owned the old suburban three-bedroom house. Before Dad died, leaving the family broke.

I deposited myself on a seat and grabbed my phone from my handbag. I had a message from my sister, KC.

No, she wasn't the lead singer of the Sunshine Band. Her name was Katherine Claire, but KC suited her.

KC – Want to hang if I drive down to Melb on Friday?

Really? She was going to drive all the way from Sydney to Melbourne? That was over ten hours on the road! My little sister, seven years younger than me, still seemed too young to have her driver's licence. But she was eighteen now and had passed her test, so I guess she could drive.

I'd always been like a second mum to KC and I

didn't like the idea of her driving all the way on her own. Anything could happen. What if she ran out of petrol halfway down the Princes Highway, surrounded by trucks? What if she was driving late at night and hit a kangaroo on the road? Or fell asleep at the wheel? I couldn't think about it.

I frowned at the screen, tapping and re-tapping a reply that wouldn't sound too overprotective and annoying. What should I say?

"Are you okay?"

I glanced up to find Christos right in front of me, standing behind a kitchen chair. He gestured to it, as if asking permission to sit with me. I nodded, he sat opposite me, watching me the whole time.

Sundry thought balloons of worry circled my head. I couldn't even articulate all the things I was worried about when it came to KC I tapped out a quick message telling her I'd call her tonight to chat.

I pressed my lips together, then told Christos a smidge of what I was feeling. "I'm fine. It's my little sister. She wants to drive all the way from Sydney to Melbourne by herself. I worry." I confided the last part in a whisper.

Christos studied my face in silence for a beat or two, then sat back and stretched his long legs to one side. He was too big for the table, like a high-school football player visiting a kindergarten class.

He crossed his arms over his massive chest. "You're

right to worry. It can be a dangerous trip, even for experienced drivers. How old is she?"

"Just eighteen."

"Yeah, I'd worry if she was my sister. I'd probably buy her a plane ticket." He scratched the back of his neck, looking super serious and super sexy. "Too many bad things can happen on the road. Too many crazy drivers."

Didn't I know it?

He didn't say it, but I'd heard he'd been a cop. The word was out through the store. Christos had been a police officer for a few years, but for some scandalous reason he'd resigned from the force and gone back to college to study law or something. So the rumours went. I wanted to ask him about it, but I didn't want to upset him and ruin our chances of being...friendly.

I put down my phone with a dull thud on the table. "I think you're right. I'll call her tonight and see if I can talk her into flying down." I tipped my head to the side and pressed my lips together. "What did you want to ask me?"

His eyes widened for a second. "Oh, right. This is kind of an odd request, but I was wondering if we could meet a few times a month. You could let me know about anything out of the ordinary you notice at work."

This was *unusual*. Could it have been an excuse to see me? But why wouldn't he just ask me out, if he was actually interested? There was my answer. He wasn't interested. He was only doing his job.

I shrugged. "Okaaay. I'm not sure what would constitute 'out of the ordinary'? Lynda being nice? Or me actually being able to create a shop display without falling on my arse?"

In my fantasy version of the incident that morning I fell on my arse behind the counter, Christos leaned over me and kissed me. Really kissed me, until I was a moaning, writhing mess on the floor. Good fantasy.

I interrupted my regularly scheduled daydreams to find Christos chuckling. His dark eyes had come alive with cheekiness. He was truly adorable. I studied his high, sculpted cheekbones and the firm line of his jaw. I may have licked my lips.

He spoke in a low, syrupy voice. It should've been bottled, like an exotic liqueur. "There's a situation I'm aware of in the store. I could use some help, if you can keep it confidential."

I nodded, but I had no idea where this was leading.

"You probably saw the commotion a while back. I had to chase some young blokes out of the store."

I leaned forward and gestured for him to continue. If Christos wanted to tell me the story, I didn't mind. He could tell me stories all day. Christos had a lovely deep voice. Calm but also commanding. It made me imagine all sorts of bedroom scenarios involving handcuffs and being under arrest... Was it hot? Did someone turn up the heating in the break room?

Christos stared at my face for a second, then cleared his throat before continuing. "Well, I apprehended them in the car park with the help of the police. We soon realised they had staff security codes and barcodes scanned on their mobile phones. They attempted to get inside the main storeroom on the ground floor. Then I spotted them."

I could see where this was headed now. Someone, a staff member, was probably helping these guys. An inside job. This was exciting. Also worrying. But exciting. "Right. Did they manage to get inside?"

He clamped his mouth shut for a second until a muscle at his jaw ticked. "Not this time. But I don't know if they'll be charged. There could be more incidents. I'm concerned there's someone giving away, or more likely, selling staff data."

Got it. Sort of. But I didn't see how I could help. "What has this got to do with me?"

He glanced at my face then down to my hands, resting close to his on the table. He sat back in his seat and huffed out a breath. "It's a big ask, but I was hoping you could keep your eyes open in the cosmetics area. There's heavy foot traffic through the department, and with staff cutbacks, we don't have a big enough security team. It can be hard to watch staff, unobtrusively."

Oh. Christos was asking me to spy on my colleagues. I'd have to think about it. After all, I'd only just started working in the store. This could potentially ruin my working life, if people got wind of the fact I was watching them or dobbing to security.

Before I could say anything else, he stood up as if to leave. "I understand if it puts you in a difficult situation. I just thought...I could trust you."

My heart thudded under the confines of my blouse, too fast for me to speak immediately. I thought there was something between us. Maybe I hadn't been imagining things for a change.

I stood too, straightening my spine. "You can trust me. I'd like to help."

I extended my right hand for him to shake, without thinking about it. Christos paused for a couple of beats, then took my hand in his. This time when we touched there wasn't only pleasant warmth and an impression of strength, there was a full-on bolt of lightning. Okay, maybe not lightning, but megawatts of electricity plus some chemical stuff mixed in. Something to do with animal attraction. It made me want to purr.

He gripped my hand tight, allowing me the privilege of treating me the same as he would a male colleague. Or not. His eyes met mine and *zing*! His look was boiling over with heat, like an unwatched pot on the stove.

With a blink and a stunned expression I'd never seen on his face before, Christos retracted his hand, quickly, as if burned.

He rubbed his hands down his sides and nodded.

"I'll let you have some lunch." And without waiting for a reply, he walked out of the room.

Right. It made me feel about as wanted as the plague and as useful as tits on a bull, as my dad used to say. I admit I stared after the retreating Christos for a moment. Where was his head at? Had I completely misread what I assumed was the simmer of mutual attraction? Did he see me as a convenient nobody he could use for his spy scheme?

I picked up my bag and strolled back through the break room towards the door just as a bunch of tech blokes from Home Entertainment and Computing strolled in.

Dressed all in black, sporting bunches of lanyards with special security access cards and passwords, they apparently thought they were it and a bit. Too cool for school. Ironic beards, hipster low-slung jeans and slicked back hair and/or spiked haircuts defined the look. They seemed to do everything together, even take lunch breaks and go to the loo. Too strange for my liking.

One of them grinned at me. Marco, who I remembered from the same staff training session Petula, Christos and I were indoctrinated in. He'd been smart as a whip in training, answering questions with ease and flirting with the thirty-something female Team Leader, Roberta. Now, he was turning his charm and his unusual caramel-coloured gaze on me.

He looked me up and down in an appreciative way, but it struck me as slimy. "Hi, Lily, isn't it?"

"Yes. How are you, Marco?"

His grin widened and I caught a glimpse of gold. A sparkly tooth on the right-hand side of his smile. "Oh, can't complain. Sold a massive surround sound system to an old dude this morning. Cha-ching! Nice little commission coming my way."

"Good work."

It seemed the right thing to say, though I couldn't pretend to be genuinely impressed. Show-off boys weren't my type. It would have been nice to have commissions in the range of thousands though. Selling perfume wasn't so lucrative for sales staff.

I made to walk off, slinging my bag over my arm. "See you later."

He tipped his head to one side and winked. "You can count on it."

With a polite smile I turned away. I pushed through the double doors. I needed to get out of there, away from all the chatty men behaving strangely. I'd get some lunch somewhere quiet and mull over my conversation with Christos.

He'd probably want me to chat to Marco and guys like him to see if anything strange cropped up. The thought was unsettling. I wasn't sure why.

Lunch beckoned. My belly growled like an angry bear as I marched through the store. I couldn't do any decent thinking on an empty stomach.

. . .

The next day was Friday, one of our biggest days of the week. Lots of women got paid on Thursdays and the money hit their bank accounts the next day. Therefore it was shopping day.

By ten o'clock the perfume counter was pumping. About eight people had been through already, purchasing bottles of scent and even one top-quality eau de parfum from the special backlit display case holding the prestigious products.

The store had purposefully upbeat dance music playing through the department's sound system, designed to put shoppers in the mood to spend, spend, spend.

I was stationed at the counter's gift wrapping table, perfecting the art of wrapping with no visible tape. I glanced up at the customer Giselle was handling. A gorgeous woman with legs like a gazelle, wrapped in a barely-there mini skirt, was chatting to Giselle. She'd been browsing when Giselle reeled her in with talk of the latest sensation from France.

"*Oui*, it is an elegant infusion of peony and honeysuckle. Sweet, but not overpowering. Subtle and distinctive. Yes?"

The customer nodded, inhaling the spritz of perfume Giselle had applied to her inner wrist. The pulse point there warmed the oils in the perfume, releasing the fragrance. It would develop on the skin, changing with the individual's chemistry.

Giselle rubbed the matching perfumed body lotion into the customer's hands, pausing to compliment her, like the pro saleswoman she was. "You have beautiful hands. Oh, and I love this nail colour!"

"It's Chanel," the customer confided.

"Of course! It is stunning." Giselle continued to give a complimentary hand massage, and the woman at the receiving end sighed. She was bound to buy all the things now. She was putty in Giselle's hands.

I turned to where Penny, one of our new casual spritzer chicks, was standing, in the middle of the main aisle through the cosmetics department. She wore a little black dress, her hair piled high on her head with a black velvet bow on top like a pair of kitten ears. She was glamorous, sexy even, but scowled like she'd just stepped in something gross on the pavement.

My heart sank. She'd got her first whiff of Heartmas the Hideous. It was hard to sell with a smile on your face when it was really rank. She sneezed, loudly.

She must have felt my eyes on her, because she looked across and caught my eye, raising one arched eyebrow in an eloquent expression. No words required. The message was along the lines of: *WTF is this?*

Just then, I yelped. "Ouch!"

Shit! I hadn't been paying attention. Blood dripped

from my thumb, so I reached across to the bench near the register and grabbed a tissue. Mopping up blood was not my favourite occupation. I couldn't stand the stuff.

Giselle and Penny dashed over to me, checking I was okay. I shook my hand in the air, trying to make the dull throb go away. Like an idiot, I'd managed to slice my thumb on the edge of the guillotine—a paper cutting machine with a sharp edge meant for rolls of wrapping paper, not fingers.

"Show me. Oh, it's a deep cut. We must find the first-aid person." Penny turned to Giselle.

Giselle bit her lip, then burst out with a flurry of words. "Christos from security. He can help. He'll fix you."

I had no doubt he could fix me, but he'd also make me swoon.

CHAPTER 5

"Ow. Ow!" I pressed my lips together and tried to retain some dignity.

I was little better than a child with a scraped knee when Christos, with his large, yet surprisingly gentle hands, swabbed my cut with sterile alcohol wipes.

"Shhh, you'll be okay." He grumbled low under his breath, as he reached for a butterfly bandage. The first-aid kit was open on the bed beside me.

Yes, *bed*.

Christos and I were sitting close together on a bed, but this wasn't quite how I'd imagined things. He was fully clothed, for one thing. Me too, but it wasn't my main preoccupation at the moment. The quiet first-aid room was small, stuffy and claustrophobic. The room reeked of antiseptic and all the vaguely threatening aromas I associated with hospitals. And blood. Not my favourites. Nope.

He applied the butterfly bandage to my poor sore thumb, and fresh scarlet oozed from the wound. Oozed. The cut was deep.

My airway closed up. I reached for my throat and undid the top two blouse buttons, taking long, slow breaths. A paper bag was thrust in front of my face and I snatched it greedily, breathing into it. Concentrating on my breath.

In, out. In, out.

Better.

My mind wandered to happier things. Puppies. Sunflowers. White chocolate and macadamia-nut cookies. Then my eyes caught Christos's steady gaze.

He ran a hand roughly through his hair. "You nearly passed out. Are you back in the land of the living?"

I winced. "Yes. It was just the…"

"Blood?"

"Mmm-hmm."

I breathed deeply. Christos didn't ask any more questions or tease me. He was just there, solid and silent, holding my hand. Wait, holding my hand? Yes, he was. To be precise, he stroked his thumb over the back of my injured hand, careful not to touch the area of the cut, now covered by the expertly applied dressing.

Christos met my gaze again and dropped my hand. He stood and glanced around the room as if searching for something. "If you're all right, I need to fill-in some paperwork. Incident report, first-aid notes."

I nodded and he crossed to the filing cabinets against the wall. I watched him and couldn't help but notice the tightness pulling at the corners of his eyes. The soft expression from a moment ago was now completely missing.

Oh well. I couldn't expect him to sit around all day playing paramedic. I shuffled forward on the bed, then lifted myself halfway to standing. My head was so woozy I plopped right back down. My vision went fuzzy, grey at the edges, so I went ahead and lay down flat on my back.

The next thing I knew Christos was at my side again. He tucked a blanket over me and passed me a glass of water. I managed to sit up enough to take a sip, then closed my eyes again. "I feel like a complete idiot."

"Why? Because you hurt yourself? You're in shock. Give yourself a break."

I opened my eyes. "Yes, boss."

He sighed and shook his head so a lock of coal black hair fell over his brows. "What am I going to do with you?"

The question raised so many possibilities in my imagination, I didn't dare speak. Luckily he did the talking.

"I'll let you rest a few more minutes, then we'll call a taxi to take you home."

"No, I'll be fine. I need to work…" I nearly told him. I only had forty dollars to my name for the rest of the week and no sick leave yet. They'd dock my pay for the hours I was on leave, reducing my income for the next week. I couldn't afford it.

Christos let out a noise of frustration from low in his throat. "Stop arguing. I'll call Hyacinth and see what she says." He unclipped his phone from his belt, punched in a number and then pressed the phone to his ear.

I groaned. Hyacinth was the floor manager, my superior in the ranking order of management at the store. In terms of actual scariness, she ranked right above Lynda. They were great mates of course, going out for drinks together after work. Probably planning new and inventive ways of torturing the staff.

Before I could panic about an imminent Hyacinth crisis, I tried to sit, leaning on my elbows. The resulting head spin wasn't a good sign.

Christos had opened the door of the small room, which suddenly seemed much smaller, like the walls were closing in on me. I didn't like the spots at the corners of my vision either.

Hyacinth poked her head through the door, scrunched up her nose at the sight of me and bustled her way inside. "She looks fine to me." She said these words with a dismissive tip of her head towards me, and directed her attention straight back to Christos.

"Lily needs to rest. She's in shock. She needs a ride home too." Christos stared her down, crossing his arms.

I was proud of him, although maybe it wasn't

appropriate to be proud of a grown man I hardly knew for standing his ground. It's just, Hyacinth was a bully and I'd never had time for bullies. Not since high school. Those days were behind me. Now I was even content with my weight. Mostly. No grown-up version of a Mean Girl was going to treat me like nothing. Even if she was technically my boss.

I closed my eyes and breathed deeply, willing myself to sink through the floor or become invisible. No such luck.

Hyacinth piped up before I could change the laws of physics. "Christos, you're due to finish your shift. Why don't you escort Lily home?" This was said with a snide smile, which spelt trouble.

Why was my snarky wench of a manager trying to get Christos to 'escort' me? What was she playing at? She was probably only trying to make me uncomfortable.

With a gracious nod and hardly a complaint, in fact I detected a faint smile playing over Christos's tempting mouth, he gestured for me to take his outstretched hand.

Willing and eager, I forgot myself and got up too quickly, the rush of blood from my top half to my bottom half making my knees shake, not in a good way. Except Christos rushed to catch me (again) before I fell at his feet (again-again).

Only this time my cheek was smooshed up to his chest, not to mention other areas pressing against the long hard length of him. The side of his body, not other regions. His arms wrapped around my waist, literally holding me up.

While he was built like a tree trunk, I was not. Curvy bits aside, I was more breakable than people imagined. But he was gentle. Even the arm gripping my waist, the hand clutching my hip. Not too hard, not too soft. Just right. Goldilocks, I was not. No way was I afraid of this big bear of a man.

I may have swooned more than necessary. I never claimed to be an uber-feminist. There was nothing wrong with a bit of flirting, in my humble opinion.

He squeezed my waist, my heart skittered, and he mumbled under his breath, "It's okay, I've got you."

Did he ever!

CHAPTER 6

❄

"Let me, please."

Christos opened the staff door for me, holding it while I gingerly walked out into the glaring mid-afternoon sunlight.

I glanced up at him and tried not to swallow my tongue. The sunlight dappling his olive-brown skin and the stubble shading his jaw made him almost irresistible. I resisted just going for it and smooching him, for now. "Thank you."

I swayed past him, not taking it too fast. I'd forgotten it was daytime. The department store building was bunker-like and I could have been in an underground cave, apart from the ever-blinding flouro lighting. I'd become accustomed. Normal light seemed alien to me now. Perhaps I was becoming a pod person. I shook my head, wishing the cobwebs away.

Christos took my arm, like a proper old-fashioned

gentleman. It was rather swoon-inducing too. It was tricky getting Christos to let me walk on my own two feet. I guessed he wanted to pick me up and haul me over his shoulder like a fireman. Part of me wanted to let him. But the rest of me, especially the part above my shoulders, noticed the small group of staff hanging around the nearby smokers' area, watching us.

Marco and crew from Home Entertainment were gathered around a high wooden table against the outside wall of my favourite café. All of them dressed in black as per usual, all of them puffing on cigarettes.

Smoking. *Urgh*. Not my chosen bad habit. I'd much prefer to kiss a man who'd been drinking coffee or even eating liquorice. Anything other than smoking. My gaze travelled straight to Christos, who closed the door and ushered me towards the car park. He wasn't a smoker.

"Lily, hey! Are you leaving so soon?" Marco's voice carried on a gust of wind that whipped the loose ends of my ponytail into my face. He sounded put out somehow.

I tilted my chin in his direction. "I'm not feeling well. Bye," I said with a tight smile, non-committal as always. I didn't want to say I'd see him tomorrow. Something about him didn't appeal to me. A frisson of warning went off in the back of my mind every time he looked me up and down. Like right now.

"Right."

Christos paused mid-stride and nodded at Marco.

"De Millo. I'll be up to talk to you tomorrow at eleven. Don't forget."

Marco mumbled something like, "Yes, officer."

Very interesting. I'd never noticed any tension between the two men before. Had I even heard them speak to each other? No. They stared at each other for an uncomfortable few seconds, before Christos tugged on my arm.

I tipped my chin up to meet his gaze. "Don't you like Marco?"

"I like him enough to work with him."

I raised an eyebrow at Christos. "Hmmm. Not really then?"

"Not in the way he likes you." His eyes wrinkled up at the corners so I wasn't sure if he was being serious.

This was interesting. I'd never noticed the way Christos's eyebrows cinched together until now. Or the way his jaw clicked when he clenched it.

We marched across the huge car park, avoiding a Mini squealing around a traffic island. Finally we made it to the undercover, multi storey monstrosity where most staff parked their cars. This was another reason I was glad to walk to work. These places creeped me out. The distinctive aroma of urine permeated the concrete stairwell. The overflowing dumpster near the wall was best left well alone.

"This is me."

So proclaimed Christos, as he clicked the electronic key to unlock a snazzy-looking sports car, not a modern deal with lots of gizmos and doohickeys, but a sleek, low to the ground 1970s number. It was deep electric blue and shiny, too. Nice. Clearly, I knew a lot about cars.

I waved my arm in the general direction of the passenger door. "*This* is very sexy. Quite the chick magnet I suppose?"

Christos cleared his throat. "It's a Monaro GTS." As if this was explanation enough.

He opened the passenger door for me. I couldn't miss the way his eyes followed the length of my stocking-clad legs all the way to my Mary Janes, but he averted his gaze as soon as I caught him staring. That look. I'd like to wrap it up with a bow and pop under the Christmas tree to enjoy later.

He let me get seated then closed the door. New car fragrance enveloped me. The combination of leather and an astringent hint of citrus reminded me of Christos. His usual scent was magnified in some way in this enclosed space. I could have happily rolled around in it for hours.

Then he was there beside me, the door snicked shut and we were sitting side by side. Together. In his car. All words deserted me, since all I could think about was the way his thighs looked splayed out in front of him.

He turned the key in the ignition while I buckled my seatbelt. The roar of the engine shook me to the core...and I mean literally. Everything in the lower half of my body vibrated and hummed with the rumble of the engine under my seat. I smoothed my hands down my skirt and kicked my handbag out of the way so I could cross my legs. Which was uncomfortable.

I shot Christos a sneaky glance under my lashes and noticed him noticing me. Again.

This time, he grinned. Hokey cliché or not, it was like the sun popping out on a cloudy day, beaming at me, radiant and sparkly.

"Ready?" he asked, but revved the engine and changed gears before I could answer.

A minute later we were out of the car park, onto the highway on one side of the shopping centre. Christos zipped and merged into the stream of traffic, while I clung to the door handle. I didn't like city traffic. Not since the accident…

"I guess I should ask you where you live." Christos broke the train of my thoughts, which were close to derailing and crashing through a level crossing.

No, no, no.

Don't think about it.

I shook my head, more vigorously than I meant to, then shook out my hands for good measure.

Christos was glancing at me, in between looking back at the road. No way was I ready to explain my aversion to traffic. Especially considering the way I'd freaked out at the sight of a little blood today. I didn't want him to label me a complete fruitcake and yet refuse to take a bite out of me.

"...or I could take you to a doctor? Get your cut looked at again? But I think it's okay. No need for stitches."

I pasted a smile on my face which strained the muscles in my cheeks. It may have actually looked more like a grimace, judging by the startled rise of Christos's eyebrows.

I pressed my lips together for a second. "I'm fine. You can drop me home. Laurinda Lane, down past the big high school. Turn left at the next intersection."

Wordlessly, Christos followed my directions. Until we got to my little street, which was a quiet, winding lane, tucked away near a park full of gorgeous old trees and walking tracks. Perfect for someone who didn't want to drive. It was only a hop, skip and jump to a tram stop or a train station too.

I nodded towards the end of the lane. "My place is down there on the left. Number 32."

He nodded, pulling up on the side of the street just near my teeny tiny front lawn and owl-shaped letter-box. I'm not sure who picked out the letterbox, a past owner I suppose, but I loved it.

"Thanks for the lift home."

Christos nodded as he killed the engine. He glanced past me to my little house. It was half a house converted to an apartment, sort of late Art Deco style with clinker bricks and cute leadlight windows beside the red painted front door. A tiny patch of lawn and a few old rosebushes faced the street near the low brick fence.

He didn't make a move to get out of the car, so neither did I. Should I kiss him? The gallumphing of my heart was enough to make me slow down and think twice. There was no need to attack the man.

I occupied my time with stressing. What if Christos wanted to come inside? I was attracted to him, no question. But was I ready to get physical if the opportunity came up? A flash of pain tore through my stomach, a pain I thought was long gone. I crossed my arms across my mid-section and breathed deep. I'd thrown myself at my ex, right after Dad died. He'd rejected me, in the cruellest way. Just thinking about it made my belly ache again.

My ex-boyfriend Scott hadn't hung around once the going got tough. He'd got off the phone as soon as he could on the most horrible day of my life, feigning a work deadline as he'd done so many times before. I'd needed him. He'd skedaddled so fast I'd had no time to adjust.

I tried to call him two days after Dad's accident, but he dumped me by text message. His behaviour wouldn't have hurt so much, except I had loved him, in my own deluded way. I was self-aware enough to understand I sometimes pushed aside the evidence of someone else's dishonesty or bad behaviour.

Scott had shown how he felt in so many ways, but if

you don't want to see it, it's not going to be obvious. Until it's all over, red rover.

A click of a seatbelt buckle pulled me back to the present moment. Christos turned to run his eyes over me. Concern was etched across his forehead in even lines.

"So, why did you leave the police force?" I didn't mean to ask the question, but it popped out of my mouth.

He chuckled under his breath, then ran his fingertips along his jaw line. A scratchy sound of friction against stubble had the tiny hairs on my arms standing on end. "Everyone knows about that, do they?"

I shrugged, squirming in my seat. I shouldn't have asked. Of course not. If I wasn't so distracted with my own past and rubbish boyfriends, I wouldn't have been so rude.

He cleared his throat. "No harm filling in the blanks. I was on the force for five years, did my job, helped people, I guess. Tried to do some good. One day my partner and I were called out to a situation. An armed robbery in progress. We should have waited for more back-up, but we were right round the corner from the jewellery store. There were five of them. Only two of us. The same guys we'd been investigating for a couple of other low-level break and enters. This time they'd upped their target."

He paused, looking straight ahead through the windscreen. "I should have known they'd take more risks with a bigger score at stake. They had a hostage. I knew her. She was an old friend, Effie. She had a gag over her mouth. When I walked in the back room of the store I saw her straight away. They knew I was coming."

I gasped, not liking where this story was going. Not one little bit. The robbers had his friend as a hostage? It was the stuff of nightmares.

Christos threaded his hands together and cracked his knuckles. "I had to get her out of there. I hit the first guy. One punch and he went down. I shot the second one. Got him in the stomach."

"Oh, no. That must have been terrible. Were you hurt?"

He nodded, then let out a slow breath. "Yeah. A bullet lodged in my knee. I had surgery, so it's okay now. Mostly. I wasn't much good for a regular beat though. A desk job at police headquarters wasn't my scene. But the security job isn't good for my knee either." He rubbed his knee absent-mindedly.

"What about Effie?"

Christos shook his head. "What happened next messed with my head. The bastard slashed her face with a knife right after I was wounded. My partner helped her, called an ambulance. But I couldn't do anything. I couldn't save her."

Now it was my turn to gasp. "Did she die?"

"No. But that bastard...he was her boyfriend. Now he's her husband."

I swung around to look him square in the face. His whole face had sagged with resignation, gone slack around his mouth.

I almost reached out and almost touched his shoulder. Almost. "You did your job. No one could ask any more."

"I asked more of myself. I failed." He stared straight ahead and didn't seem to see me at all.

Before I knew what I was doing, or before I freaked out about a man not liking me as much as I liked him, as per usual, I reached out and placed my hand over his. The hand now resting on his thigh.

He shifted, moving towards me, coming closer. So close I was inside his wrap-around layer of warmth, his addictive scent drawing me in.

His body whispered to mine: *closer, closer.*

Mine whispered in response: *yes please, yes please.*

His lips met mine, first touching with a brush of his lips, then more fully owning my mouth. I opened my lips, just a touch. His tongue brushed mine, just a taste. His hands were on my hips, gripping me, squeezing me, not too tight, just right. He groaned into my mouth.

A noise rose out of my chest like *harrumph*, and I knew. This man could kiss me all day long and never get tired of it, or complain I was boring. He wouldn't call me too needy or greedy. Christos was greedy for my kisses and I loved it.

My heart pounded away like a disco diva on the

dance floor. The song playing low on the radio swirled through my mind, a great track. *Heart of Glass* by Blondie. All I could think was...finally. Finally I'd found him.

Then, what the hell? *Clunk.* My knee connected with the gearstick in the centre console and I yelped. I leaped away from Christos as if I'd been stung by a bee. I bit my lower lip, which was suddenly swollen.

The man could kiss. But should I invite him inside? In the middle of the afternoon? Before we'd even been out to dinner? I was apparently becoming a kiss first, ask questions later kind of woman.

These dilemmas never usually happened to me. I'd normally be lucky to get a hint of interest somewhere down the road, after the third or fourth date. Too many blokes gave me the whole 'you're a great girl, but let's be friends' speech at that point.

I flicked my gaze to Christos's face. His eyes fixed on my face in intense concentration. On my lips, truth be told. A thrilling development.

He shifted sideways so he could look me straight in the eyes. "I've been wanting to kiss you since the day in training when you fell into my arms."

Oh, boy. Had he really been scoping me out the way I'd been (ever so sneakily) checking him out? How should I respond? "Really? Um, thank you."

He chuckled. "No, thank you. You're a beautiful woman. Brave and smart too."

Heat rose to my cheeks until I'm sure they were

painted as red as my hair. "You're a flatterer. But as my gran used to say, flattery will get you everywhere."

Everywhere?

I shouldn't have said that. I was a complete nong. He probably thought I was a rampant man-eating bonk-aholic. Which was so far from the truth I didn't even know where to start digging myself out of the conversational hole.

Christos simply smiled in his sparkly way. He reached for my hand. The injured hand. I'd completely forgotten about it. He held my fingers gently, stroking his thumb across the underside of my palm in such a way...random sparks of fabulousness shot straight to my much-neglected Female Zone. It was capitalised in my mind in much the same way as an unexplored region on a half-drawn map of the world long ago. It might have been marked: Uncharted Territory or There Be Dragons.

Christos let go of my hand and sighed. "I'd better get you inside. I have to get going too. Family dinner."

It was funny how a good kiss could distract you from pain. Or completely rattle you, so you forget what you were doing sitting in a virtual stranger's car. Except Christos didn't feel like a stranger. Not anymore. Maybe he never did.

I sucked in a breath and grabbed my handbag. "Come in for a coffee?"

He hesitated, but only for a microsecond. "Sure, I'd love to."

CHAPTER 7

❄

"Come in." I opened the front door, giving it a swift kick because it was old. The wood panel tended to jam in the frame.

Christos was right behind me, and I mean right up close. I thought he was going to touch me, maybe place his hand on the small of my back in the shiver-inducing way I liked. But no such luck.

I heard a noise. A random note of a keyboard, over and over. My housemate was home.

It was a pity I had to share the house, at least some of the time. Luckily he travelled a lot for work, being a musician, so I didn't see him often. Our schedules were opposite, since I worked mostly days and he worked mostly nights. So we didn't actually see much of each other and we each had a sense of privacy. Except neither of us brought anyone home. Not anyone who might stay overnight, at least.

This could be awkward. I closed the door behind us, Christos craning his neck towards the bedroom down the hall. He'd obviously heard the noise too.

"Sorry, I didn't know he'd be here. Bill usually works nights so I don't see him much."

He cleared his throat. "That must be difficult."

"Not really. It's not like we hang out together all the time. Except when we go to bed. This place is our crash pad, I suppose."

Christos's eyebrows shot up, his whole body tensed, like he'd gone into fight-or-flight mode. He was acting weird, for sure. "I better get going. Mum's expecting me. Family dinner, you know."

I didn't try to hide the disappointment from my voice. "Oh, okay. If you really have to go…"

He nodded, already heading for the door. "I really have to go."

"Let me just get you a coffee. After all…" Should I mention the kiss? My instincts shouted a definite, *NO!* See what happens, don't mention it, don't try for a date or hookup. Not yet. I didn't want to jinx it. "You helped me. Fixing up my hand, and giving me a ride home."

Christos stopped and stared at me for a second. Stared through me, since his attention seemed to be caught by the same note of the keyboard, echoing down the hall. "Glad to help. See you at work, Lily."

He slammed the door behind him, the sound marking time like the end of something. An episode of my romantic life, cut short, before it even got to the good bits. Before he got to see my good bits.

I sagged against the door and let out a noise of my own. Pure frustration, plus a healthy dose of confusion. What had got into Christos all of a sudden?

Then Bill poked his head through the bedroom door, where he was clearly visible, standing near his keyboard. Wearing only a too-small blue towel slung around his hips. Otherwise naked.

Not exactly the impression I was going for. Christos must have seen him. *Oh no!*

Christos thought I had an older, hairier, musician layabout housemate/boyfriend. This was only partly the truth.

In actual fact, I had an older, hairier, musician layabout *uncle,* soon to move to the US and sublet his house to me for bargain-basement rent. Uncle Bill was the cool one in the family. He never stuck around much when I was a kid, but now he was coming through for me.

I was grateful to Bill, truly. Just not at that exact moment.

This wasn't good. Not good at all. Christos would hate me now.

Kissing him one minute, leading him into my love nest with half-naked older dude the next.

Bill lifted one hand in a friendly wave. "Hi there, kiddo. How was work?"

I sighed, and even to my own ears I sounded a

hundred years old. "Oh, fine. Except for the part when it was a disaster." I shuffled into the living room, kicked off my high heels and dumped my bag on the coffee table. My bottom landed in the centre of the green velvet sofa.

I held up my bandaged hand for Bill's benefit. "I had a little accident. Wrapping presents, would you believe?"

Bill shook his head, his greying hair escaping from his hippie-style ponytail at the nape of his neck. "Ah, kiddo. That's rough. Let me make you a coffee. White with one, right?"

I sank down into the sofa cushions and closed my eyes. "Right. But make it a glass of wine. A large one, thanks."

T he next few days sailed by as if I'd never even met, let alone kissed a man named Christos. When I say sailed by, the days sailed along smoothly, but the nights were full of choppy seas and undertows, with strange dreams pulling me under. Waking memories of Christos kissing me left me shaken up. By day I was going through the motions and sighing.

Today was no different. I sat at the low table behind the perfume counter, adding up our weekly sales against targets. Doing busy work, in other words.

Christos was avoiding me. I tried to catch his attention, glancing up from my mind-numbing book work and waving at him across the floor. I even succeeded in getting him to look at me. He looked back blankly, as if he didn't know who I was. Or didn't want to know. Then he marched off in the opposite direction.

I stared at his departing back as he exited the floor for the staff corridor. He wouldn't even give me a chance to explain. That hurt most. Like I wasn't worth his time or effort.

I was more alone than ever. I felt it down to my toes, dressed up snazzily in my new black and white two-tone Jazz style shoes. But not even fancy new shoes I couldn't afford could improve my gloomy mood.

Petula had tried to cheer me up. She'd invited me out to dinner with herself and Kurt last night. I'd politely declined. The whole third-wheel thing, watching them so happy together, wasn't going to help.

Giselle also tried to brighten my day, telling me stories about her last trip to Paris and how she'd visited an actual perfume blender. She stood beside the counter, polishing the glass counter tops. It was a slow day. We'd served a few customers but it wasn't exactly exciting.

With a sigh, Gisele tossed her long ponytail behind her shoulder. "I wish you would come to Paris with me. I would show you all the special places only locals know. You could stay with me and my aunt in her apartment. It is beautiful, one of my favourite places in the world."

"It sounds wonderful."

The way she described the perfumery, the neighbourhood on the left bank of the Seine, the aromas when you entered the main salon, it made me yearn.

It made me want to run away to Paris, immediately. Which of course was impossible. Mainly because I needed money. Also because I couldn't just up and leave the country, completely leaving my sister to her own devices. It was bad enough I'd left her alone in Sydney. Well, with friends, but she didn't have me. It was only for a while, until I could get her enrolled in university. I had to be her support, her lifeline. And I wanted her to have a future.

Giselle put down her polishing cloth and turned to me. "I wish we could go. Next year. Paris in springtime. One day we will. We might be old ladies, but we'll go."

I laughed, even though it wasn't funny. Giselle couldn't take off for Paris either, not in the near future. Her parents were here in Melbourne and they were getting older. They depended on her.

Next thing I knew, Petula was speed-walking across the floor towards the perfume counter. The manicure bar was no busier than our area. "Hey, are you girls on for drinks after work tonight? Unofficial Christmas party. We're going to Granite Bar."

"Who's we?"

"Oh, me and Kurt, some of the make-up team, the fashion crew, Christos…"

I held up a hand in a stop-sign motion. "Stop right

there. Back up a bit. Christos is going out with the girls?"

Petula leaned on the edge of our counter and drummed her amazing fingernails on the glass. They were hot pink with a swirly pattern today. She blinked at me. "It's not just girls. Kurt will be there. Plus Marco and the guys from upstairs."

Okay. Maybe Petula didn't organise this last-minute party to force Christos and I together. Maybe. The jury was still out about her motives in organising the shindig. But it wasn't like I had any better offers. "Sure, I'll stop by. If I'm not too tired."

Giselle nodded, then stepped forward, standing as close to Petula's position as she could get. "Will Peter Harrison be there?"

Hello, this was news. Giselle was asking about Mr Harrison, the elusive store manager. Since when was she interested in silver-fox type men? Since Mr Harrison, perhaps?

He existed. I'd seen him a few times, but he wafted around on the executive level upstairs and didn't make his presence known on the cosmetics floor. Giselle had never seemed particularly interested in him, until now.

Petula's eyes twinkled. It could have been a trick of the light or her gold glittery eyeshadow, but I suspected not. Mischief was afoot in Petula-land. "I could invite him, if you like. I know when he takes his coffee break at the place in the mall."

Giselle rolled her eyes, ducking behind the counter

to refill the display cabinets. "I don't care. What does it matter to me?"

Petula and I locked eyes and tried not to laugh. I was more successful than she was.

Petula giggled like a schoolgirl. "Great. I'll see you two ladies tonight. And I expect you both to look absolutely rock-star hot."

R*ock-star hot.*
Glancing down at my outfit, I did a quick inventory. I wasn't sure if it quite fit the bill, but it would have to do. I smoothed my hands down my dress in the back seat of the car. My favourite vintage 'wiggle dress' à la Marilyn Monroe was a satiny fabric in scarletty-pink. *Spink?* It fitted me like a second skin.

It was my best lady-on-the-town look, complete with high heels that made my legs look fifty miles long, but also made it difficult to walk anywhere. So I'd taken an Uber to the bar. I adjusted my dress and my victory-roll hairdo as I climbed out of the car and said goodnight to the nice grandma-like driver.

When I waddled inside Granite Bar it was dark, but I could make out some details. The walls were painted the deepest shade of purple I'd ever seen outside a Prince music video. The music was pulsing, a deep bass thrumming underfoot and rattling the glassware on the tables.

The gang was all there, mostly. Petula, gorgeous as

ever in a silver halter top and black mini skirt, the smitten Kurt by her side, his hair sticking up on top like a parrot's. A few of Marco's crew were hanging around, sipping beers as they leaned against the bar. They were all dressed in black as usual, and blended into the background.

I waved at Petula, who'd seen my entrance, and I made my way inside, pushing past throngs of people sipping cocktails. It was Happy Hour so loads of office groups were here for the discount drinks. The scent of fake raspberry wafted by as I walked past a group of younger women drinking frozen margaritas.

Petula signalled for me to come over. I nodded. Some random man behind me wolf-whistled as I walked. I kept right on walking and rolled my eyes. Petula giggled, her shoulders shaking as she sipped her drink.

I didn't see Christos. Not that I was looking for him. Still, I couldn't help scoping out the remaining seats nearby.

A whole group of make-up chicks from the cosmetics counters were lined up along a low leather bench. They were glamorous as always, but they couldn't compete with Giselle, sitting on her own in a suitably chic black leather armchair.

My French friend was checking her phone and had her legs crossed to one side. Her little black dress was covered in tiny sequins, so she shimmered whenever the overhead light hit her. A deliberate choice, I'd bet.

Just like her choice of prime position with a clear view of the door.

She was waiting for someone. My money was on our mysterious store manager. I didn't think it was likely he'd show up tonight, but what did I know? Stranger things had happened. Giselle raised her head and smiled at me, then returned to scrolling on her phone screen.

Finally, I skirted around a wooden coffee table and took a seat to the right of Petula, with Kurt on her left. He had his arm around her shoulders in a casual way.

"Hey, Lily, you look soooo sexy. Doesn't she look sexy, Kurt?" Without waiting for an answer, Petula chatted on. "I'm looking forward to seeing if *someone* makes an appearance." She nodded meaningfully at me.

"Oh, you mean Peter Harrison? Giselle's waiting for him, I think."

Petula goggled at me, eyes wide. "No, not him! I mean Christos. He said he might pop in on his way to his grandmother's place. Isn't that sweet?"

Yes, he was sweet. I'd have to try not to overindulge in thoughts of him or I'd rot my teeth. He'd obviously been avoiding me and I didn't want a man who didn't want me. Or who only put up with me until someone better/thinner/richer came along. Been there, done that, got the t-shirt.

So why was I watching the door?

I didn't even notice Marco until he was right in front of me, pink margarita in hand. "Here you go.

Couldn't help noticing the drink matches your dress. Nice."

My lips twitched. It wasn't quite a smile. "Thank you. How are you?"

He bounced on the balls of his feet, hands stuffed in his pockets. He didn't have a drink of his own. "Oh, I'm great. Just got the prototype of my app up and running."

I didn't have the faintest clue about what to say to this guy. He was into IT stuff, I was into perfume. I didn't think we clicked. But maybe I'd missed the point…

"It sounds interesting. What does your app do exactly?" Petula was gazing up at Marco from under her embellished eyelashes. I hadn't noticed Kurt walk away, but he must have done.

Marco stood opposite us and preened his hair. The way he stood in such a purposefully laid-back way had to be for show. I may not be an IT genius, but I was a good judge of body language. Marco was one-hundred-and-ten per cent into Petula but trying not to show it.

He sidled up to her now and sat beside her. Not too close, but not miles away. He grabbed his smartphone and showed her something on screen. "It's a booking app for bands for Italian-speaking users. I think there's a big market for people booking bands for weddings and parties, and they can listen to a sample of the songs and read the reviews."

He said something about the iTunes store and user testing. I zoned out.

Petula, for her part, was fluttering and flirting like she meant it. She touched his forearm and I felt my eyebrows pop up somewhere near my hairline. I may not have been a math expert either, but I was certain she was more than one-hundred-and-fifty per cent into Marco. Why hadn't I noticed this earlier? What else had I been missing?

I took a few sips of my drink as I half-listened to their conversation. I hadn't known either of them for long, so it was no wonder I didn't understand what was going on with them. Or what they might have been hiding from me.

Petula and Marco were deep in conversation when Giselle pulled her chair up next to me. She was talkative again now.

"You know how I said we should go to Paris next year? Perhaps it will happen. I don't know. I think..." she paused, glancing up at me. Her eyes had a suspiciously red-tinge, now I had a close-up view, "I think we will be moving back to France. My parents wish to go home and they need me."

Earlier, I would have thought this would have been cause for celebration in Giselle's world. But she didn't seem ready to pop any Champagne corks or start singing *La Marseillaise*.

"You don't want to go?"

Giselle closed her eyes and took a moment to

answer. "I don't know. I have not lived in France full-time since I was fifteen. Australia is my home now."

As Giselle was reminiscing, telling me her memories of going to school in Paris, something tugged at me from deep in my brain. Or my senses, I wasn't too sure. All I knew was the tiny hairs on the back of my neck and on my arms stood on end, an awareness of something, *someone*, pinged with my most visceral animal self, waking it from slumber until it was ready to purr.

I raised my head and glanced at the bar's entrance, and I think my mouth popped open. There he was. Christos was holding the door for a couple of women entering ahead of him, because of course he was. He was a true gentleman. Dressed in a fine suit, he was also a genuine lady-killer. *Purrrr...*

I had to get myself under control. I shifted in my seat and crossed my legs tight together. Just because Christos was wearing a slim-fitting grey silk suit and a white shirt unbuttoned a few notches, revealing a nice tufty bit of chest hair, was no reason to roll over and mewl like a pussycat. Or to ask him to scratch my belly.

So, I had an itch that needed scratching. It wasn't his fault. He probably didn't even want to talk to me. Except...maybe I was wrong. Dead wrong.

He glanced in my direction and did a cartoonish double take, literally turning his head away then whipping it back, front and centre, to lock eyes with me. His smouldering hot chocolate eyes had gone liquidy-melty and were practically pouring all over my body.

Oh, yes please.

He let the door close behind him and slithered towards me. Yes, slithered. It was something about his suit, it gave him a snake-like skin. And he knew I was watching him. I knew he knew, because of the way his lips quirked up at one corner. I knew that he knew that I knew... He swivelled his hips to get past a group of guys, and I lost my train of thought.

Petula elbowed me in the ribs. "It's Christos! He's here. Act naturally," she almost shouted. I rolled my eyes at her, letting my gaze leave the man I wanted to watch.

Then he was there in front of me and I had some kind of wonderful full-body shiver. He was staring down at me. Quite frankly, he shouldn't have been allowed to use that look in public. Because I suddenly wanted to rip all my clothes off and climb Christos like a tree.

He stuffed his hands into his pants pockets and I struggled to remain focused on his face, like a lady. Certain regions of his body were at my eye level from where I sat. I've never been a full-on man candy aficionado until now. But I wanted this man's candy.

He cleared his throat. "Hi, Lily."

"Christos." I nodded, keeping calm and composed, on the outside. "It's good to see you." I noted the frostiness in my own voice and crossed my legs a little tighter. It was up to him if he wanted me defrosted. A little bit of warmth from him would go a long way to thawing me out.

He extended his hand to me. "Would you like to dance?"

I tipped my head to the right and examined him, outstretched hand and all. Dancing with Christos was pretty high on my Must Do list. In fact *he* was at the top of my Must Do list. But the music in this gin joint was average at best, verging on terrible.

Only Mr David Bowie took over, a familiar tune playing from the speakers. I wasn't the only one in the bar to crack a grin. *Let's Dance*, indeed. It was a good omen.

So I grabbed Christos's hand and let him haul me up from my seat. No need to keep the man in suspense. "I'd bloody well love to dance with you. Come on." I tugged on his hand, pulling him towards the dance floor.

I'd cracked him up. He laughed low and in my opinion, dirty. I vaguely heard Petula laughing herself into a coughing fit as we made our way to the small dance floor.

Christos squeezed my hand and I nearly fell off my high heels. He took the lead now, weaving through the crowd and saying 'excuse me' to millions of people before we found some room to manoeuvre.

This place was primarily a watering hole, but they sometimes rented the whole bar for parties. So there was a dance floor complete with mirror ball, but it wasn't ginormous. Still, there was no good reason why Christos had to pull me so close, right up to his body so we were smooshed together. No reason at all why he had to place his hand so possessively on my lower back, inching towards my butt. No reason. Except all the best reasons.

I tipped my head up (he was impressively tall, now I was up close) to meet the man's gaze. His gaze flicked up to mine just a beat or two after I caught him staring down my cleavage. This was to be expected. My boobs, after all, were imposing, in the manner of mountains with a great valley between. His cheeks now held a hint of rosy colour which made me giggle.

He sighed. "I'm so glad I came out tonight. Petula told me I had to, or else."

My giggling burbled out, full blown. "Or else what?"

He opened his eyes wide in mock horror. "I didn't want to find out. She can be scary at times."

With a snort, I laughed even harder. Until Christos interrupted.

"I had to see you. Petula told me you're living in your uncle's house. He was the one I saw the other day."

He left it there, but I knew what else he wanted to say. Bill wasn't who he'd thought. He wasn't my sugar-daddy or anything so gross. I was just a grown woman living with my adult uncle...urgh, still kind of gross when I thought about it. I couldn't wait for Bill to take off for America, then the place would be mine alone.

I tipped my head to the right and let him see a touch of the annoyance I'd felt when he'd run out on me. I raised one eyebrow. "I would have explained if you'd hung around. But you shot out of there like a bat out of hell. I haven't got anything to hide."

A charming crinkle formed in the space between Christos's eyebrows. I wanted to lick it. "I'm sorry I jumped to the wrong conclusion. It's...happened before. A woman I was seeing, two-timing me. I couldn't go through it again."

"So don't do it again. Don't run off without talking to me."

He nodded. "Okay."

Silently, I nodded too, and linked my hands around the back of his neck. I was dying to ask about the woman who'd hurt him. Whether she was pretty. Or skinny. If she was the sort of woman who stomped all over men because she could. I knew nothing about her and hated her already. But the music infiltrated my bones and muscles, relaxing me. Or it could have been the way Christos pulled me infinitesimally tighter to his hard body. We swayed together, just as Bowie suggested. Lucky I had my red shoes on too.

I deliberately kept up the chatter, in case I followed my earlier impulse and simply climbed the man. "Anyway, my uncle's moving to the US soon. He's a session musician and he's got a regular gig at a studio in LA. I'll be renting his house for the next year, at least."

"And then?"

I let out a long breath, deflating as I spoke. "Move back to Sydney, I suppose."

For the first time, I thought about moving back to Sydney and my heart hit my shoes, or roundabouts. I'd thought it was what I wanted. Sydney had always been home. But maybe it was time for new plans. "I might stay here, I don't know yet. It depends. I'm filling in for the perfume counter manager who's on maternity leave. And then there's my sister. I want her to come down to Melbourne for university."

Christos listened to every word out of my mouth, intently. To be the object of his focus, his gaze, it was pleasant. Warm. Okay, the heat in my blood was almost volcanic, and it also threatened to make me pass out.

"You could stay in Melbourne then." As he drew out the words, he stroked his fingertips over the small of my back, making me shiver.

I covered my reaction with a shrug. "Maybe. Life is full of possibilities."

Christos's laugh was like liquid, rushing and pouring over my hormone-addled body. I could've drowned in his laugh, or the tone of voice he used when he spoke low in my ear, only for me to hear.

"You always smell amazing," Christos bent his head, nuzzling close to my ear. "Like a whole garden in spring."

Hello, jelly legs.

Lucky he was holding me close because otherwise I would've slid straight onto the floor. As it was, he grabbed me in a complicated low down rock 'n' roll jive. It was impressive. And ranking somewhat dirty on the Dirty Dancing scale.

As he pulled me back up to standing, I rocked back in my heels. I assumed I had permission to sniff his throat in return, so I took full advantage. "Right back at ya. Spice, cardamon, hint of amber. Unusual fragrance."

"I don't think you can get it here. Bought it in Greece last summer."

Oh, now I was picturing him swimming in the turquoise waters off the coast of some exotic Greek island. Tanned skin shimmering with silvery droplets of water in the sunshine. An image that was doing naughty things to my hips, as they undulated against him, without my prior permission. Not to mention my nipples straining against the fabric of my lacy bra and my silky dress. It was both excruciating and smouldering hot.

Excruci-hot.

Hold on, brain. Get control now. I need you.

I must have said something out loud or at least made a grunt, because Christos responded. "Let's get out of here. Did you drive?"

"No, I got an Uber."

A frown marred Christos's brow and a lock of super shiny black hair flopped over his forehead. "They're not safe. You don't know who you're getting with those drivers. I'll give you a ride home, if it's cool with you."

I ran my fingertips down his arm. "I'm pretty good at taking care of myself. But I'm cool as a cucumber. No, cool as ice-cream. Or an iceberg. Or a penguin."

Christos barked out a laugh, more of a cough really, and offered me his arm. He ushered me towards the front of the bar. "Come on, Happy Feet. Waddle this way."

CHAPTER 8

Christos's motor was running, rumbling under my bottom. Really, it wasn't as dirty as it sounded. But as we approached my house in his cool car, all the fun thoughts fled. There were lights on in the front windows.

There had to be a law against it. *Men.*

Well, not men in general, but my Uncle Bill. Especially Uncle Bill being home when I desperately wanted him to be out. Why couldn't he be boozing with his mates at the local pub tonight? No, he had to be responsible all of a sudden, at home, packing for his trip even though there was still nearly two weeks to go.

Two weeks. Not so long in the grand scheme of things.

Only it was an eternity when I had ants in my pants, and an enormous, hot, manly man right beside me, eager to get itching. Or into my itchy pants? *Eww.*

Uncle Bill's untimely presence was even ruining the sexy euphemisms popping into my head. Even if the sentiment was true. I crossed my legs, uncomfortably aware of how I'd worked myself up just by thinking about being alone with Christos.

Christos had pulled up outside my house. It was nearly dark and the lights were clearly on inside the house. More unexpected were the extra cars and motorbikes lined up along the curb, even on our small patch of front lawn. In the quiet cul-de-sac, it was obvious we had visitors.

"Oh no." I twisted the end of my hair around my fingertip. A bad habit from childhood when I was stressed. I didn't need the split ends or the frazzled nerves.

"What's the matter?" But Christos likely knew, or guessed something in the correct vicinity. I watched him clock the vehicles on either side of the street. "Is your uncle having a party?"

A sigh rose up out of my throat and it was tinged with trepidation. "So it seems, unfortunately. I'm sorry. I thought we'd be alone…"

Christos reached for me, smoothing his thumb across my lower lip. "Come on. I'll walk you inside."

I didn't know what to make of his bland, gentle-man-like comment. He wanted to walk me inside, but did he want to come in? Even if my uncle was having an aging hippie-rocker blowout inside? My brain was stuck in first gear because Christos had touched my lips. He must have set off a chain reaction in my body, because random parts of me were trembling.

Christos was out of his door and had rounded the car to open my door before I had a chance to think it through. What if I introduced Christos to Bill? What was the worst that could happen?

The worst could be pretty bad. Bill fancied himself as a stand-up comedian as well as a muso. If he had a few drinks under his belt plus a microphone, he'd be a menace to prospective boyfriends everywhere. Bill had been known to eviscerate strangers from the safety of a stage. In his own house maybe he'd show some restraint. Maybe.

Anyway, when had I started thinking of Christos as a prospective boyfriend? Who was I kidding? He'd slotted into the category since the first moment he volunteered as tribute during our retail training, and he caught me when I fell into his yummy strong arms.

Yep. The moment had emblazoned itself on my brain forever. And possibly my heart.

I took Christos's offered hand and let him help me out of the car. His touch was hot, but not scorching. It was reassuring, not to mention sure and steady. Unlike my legs.

I clambered onto my high heels like they were roller skates, nearly losing my footing and meeting the concrete pavement face first, up close and personal.

"You've got to stop falling at my feet, Lily." Christos pulled me up with ease, chuckling at his own joke.

"You don't really want me to stop, do you?" I squeezed his arm through his shirt sleeve.

He tensed. His face blanked. I felt my face scrunch into a frown because Christos didn't look like potential boyfriend Christos all of a sudden. He looked like dead-serious-security-guard Christos.

He glanced sideways at me, still poker-faced. "Have you been putting on a show to get my attention? Because I'm not into games, Lily."

My eyes popped open and I stopped walking. "What? No, I was joking. But I'm not usually so clumsy. I can only assume you have a sex-bomb, anti-gravity effect on me."

His expression relaxed, then a slow, cheeky smile spread across his face. "In that case, I like having an effect on you."

Without warning, he reached for my hand and placed it on his chest. The rapid beat of his heart beneath the thin fabric of his shirt, the rhythmic, *da-dum, da-dum*, like a drum beat.

He moved closer, speaking next to my ear, making my own heart speed as his breath danced across my skin. "You have an effect on me too. You make me want to take a risk…"

Whatever he was going to say next was drowned out by the crash of cymbals and the beat of actual drums from inside my living room. I glanced up at Christos, his dark eyes like pools of inky night sky, dripped down from above. His pupils were dilated and

I wanted to drag him into my bedroom like a cavewoman.

Instead, I invited him to join the mad carnival of Bill's world, and mine. "Come inside. I'll introduce you to Uncle Bill. He's a riot."

I winked, letting him know there was more to discover. But I'd let him draw his own conclusions. Chances are, he'd get scared off and never come back. More than one person had labelled Bill a freak, and me by association. My belly muscles constricted at the thought, and it wasn't the cavewoman part of me this time.

Christos took my hand and led me to my own front door.

My head didn't stop turning with conflicting thoughts. As my heels click-clacked on the concrete path, I debated my own reactions.

I knew without a doubt I wanted Christos. Wanted, craved, fantasised about daily. Hourly. It was a concern, for a woman with short-term plans. This city, this job, this house—it was all temporary.

I suspected my feelings for Christos weren't temporary at all. Loving him could be a full-time occupation.

I unlocked the door with a shaking hand, nervousness overtaking me. Christos was right behind me, so warm. He was like a radiator, and the spring weather was already sticky.

The drum beat intensified as I *creeeaked* open the door, then the strains of guitar hit. When we passed over the threshold, I knew the exact moment Christos spotted Uncle Bill in his full regalia. The man now beside me stopped still, but the man in the swing of a guitar solo, my semi-famous drag queen uncle, was grinning.

Bill's red lipstick was crooked again. I'd have to talk to him about the new range of long-wearing matte lipsticks we had in store. Seriously. It ruined the effect of his stunning and slinky red sequinned dress, and of course the trademark fishnet tights and knee high boots. But the glam blonde wig set off the whole look. The Marilyn-esque hairdo was gorgeous.

Bill, or should I say, Regina, stopped playing. So did his sidekick on drums, Barry, aka Stella, who was decked out in punk-rock-chick style. The look was working for him.

I cleared my throat and hoped the evening wasn't about to go for a U-turn to awkward-land. "Hey, Bill, I'd like you to meet Christos. My new...friend. From work."

"Welcome! Take a seat. If you can find one." Bill waved us inside and I finally scoped out the rest of the room.

An assortment of characters were strewn about my living room, including a few old faces. I spotted Dad's old on-again, off-again girlfriend, Carrie. She smiled and waved hello, while ushering me to sit down.

I plonked myself down on the small armchair beside her and Christos hovered next to me. I shuffled over and he grinned, squeezing into the gap next to me.

"I didn't know there would be a floor show. I would have visited weeks ago."

Then I knew it would be all right. Christos was cool with the weirder elements of my small family. I reached over and squeezed his knee. Then bit my lip. Because I actually wanted to leap into his lap and kiss him until my head was spinning and I felt his hardness under me. But it probably didn't need to be a floor show.

Bill struck a few chords on his guitar again, then a couple more members of the group rose to the makeshift stage area in front of the fireplace. Then they were into an up-tempo version of Led Zeppelin's *Stairway to Heaven*, an old favourite. I reckon I must have watched the music show on TV about a million times, with all the hundreds of cover versions of Stairway. It was a part of my childhood.

"They're really good. How do they play so well, impromptu?" Christos asked, turning to me a second after he spoke. "Hey, it's okay." He reached for my face and wiped his thumb across each of my cheeks.

My own hand went to my cheeks and found my skin damp. Tears. I hadn't even realised. Dad had loved this song, and the flashes of him playing keyboard and piano at home, along with Bill, and me and KC running around dressed in black and playing roadies, swooshed through my head in a rush. Because this had been Dad's band once.

This time I did clamber into Christos's lap, and I liked the way he groaned under his breath and clenched his jaw. His stubbly jaw, which I so desperately wanted to run my fingertips along and feel the friction. There was a whole load of friction I wanted to feel with this man.

When I looked up and zoned into what was going on around me, Bill's eyebrows waggled in my direction even as he strummed his guitar. He mouthed the word 'handsome' and grinned, his pearly whites glinting. Then he turned his attention inward, falling into the music as he so often did.

Christos, meanwhile, had his hand on my hip again. It was distracting in the absolutely best way. There was no denying the attraction between us anymore. It zinged and zipped in the space around us like the swooping, soaring notes of the music. No longer so in control, I snuggled back against him and there it was. Unmistakable proof—Christos wanted me too.

Hooray, halleluiah and hello, handsome!

I'd picked it, picked him, almost from the first moment I saw him. My body had known. He was half hard, sitting here in a room full of people he didn't know, because I was close to him. I didn't even want to shift my legs, in case I made the situation more inconvenient. Because it was bloody inconvenient.

Why couldn't we have gone back to his place? An interesting thought.

"Later we can go back to my place." It wasn't a question, the way it was rumbled out on a huff of breath, low enough so no one else could hear.

Clearly, the man was psychic. Or else my body was giving off so many 'take me' signals, I didn't require subtitles. No words at all.

"Uh-huh," I breathed. I was clearly a conversational genius.

I couldn't focus on my surroundings. The music had stopped, but the beat of my heart thundered on. Around me, a bunch of guys I didn't know, sitting on the floor, clapped and whistled as Bill took a bow.

I couldn't focus on anything but the urgent need to be with Christos, right now thank you. I know what I want, just ring it up. I don't need any fancy gift wrapping. Because the customer is always right, after all.

Bill was probably an evil wizard putting a curse on my love life, because suddenly he announced my presence. "Hello to my niece, Lily, who's house-sitting for me while I'm in the US. She's going to be the queen of her own perfume empire one day. What you might not know is she's a talented singer, like James back in the day."

I shut my eyes and willed him to stop talking. No such luck. Evil wizard he was.

"I'm sure she wouldn't mind jamming with us old

folks and getting some air in those lungs of hers. Up you come."

"No." I shook my head.

I didn't need another crying incident with all of these people looking at me. It all reminded me too much of Dad, James. He'd been a fine singer and Bill was only trying to be friendly. I didn't need to put myself in an uncomfortable spot for him.

The applause was overwhelming though. My fingers shook as I smoothed them down my thighs, erasing non-existent wrinkles from the lower half of my silky dress.

Christos shifted, and I didn't think I could take it if he forced me to get up there. "Lily, is this okay with you? You don't have to sing if you don't want to."

Then Carrie leaned over close to my right hand side. Her greying blonde hair hung loose and wavy around her shoulders and she pushed it back with one hand. "I always loved your voice, Lil. Why don't you sing us a tune? Then you two can nick off somewhere quiet." She rubbed my shoulder and the simple gesture was fortifying somehow.

"What about a Blondie tune?"

I heard myself say the words before I knew what the hell I was doing. I had been known to jump in at the deep end, even if I only knew how to doggy-paddle. What did I really have to lose?

Bill looked fit to burst with excitement. He actually

bounced on the balls of his feet. "Of course, kiddo. *Heart of Glass?*"

So, I found my legs moving. I found myself standing in front of a microphone in my living room, before a miscellaneous crowd of bikers, old-school hippies, cross-dressing rockers, plus Bill's mates from the local pub. And Christos.

Christos, who was currently running his hungry gaze over me, like I was chocolate sauce he wanted to pour on ice-cream, maybe with whipped cream. Like he'd devour me whole. Heat rose from the pit of my stomach to the roots of my hair. If I wasn't blushing as deep as my scarlet dress, I'd be mighty surprised. Shockingly, I didn't care.

I let out the opening lyrics of the song, then fell into rhythm with Bill and the gang, swaying my hips and bobbing my head to the pop beat. I sang only for one person in the room. And the words floated in the air, about an old love and a new one, a fragile heart made of glass and hoping for more.

The real thing.

CHAPTER 9

❄

This time in the car with Christos, I didn't just have ants in my pants. I thought I'd actually expire. My clothes had effectively become a boa constrictor, cutting off all the air to my lungs, squeezing me tight, stopping the blood circulating. My pulse thudded wildly in several important places.

Clothes. Who needed them? *Bah, humbug!* They needed to come off, and soon. I tugged at the low neck-line of my dress.

As we drove towards his place, my own heartbeat was amplified in my ears, loud as the thrum of rain on a tin roof. Like the annex of my gran's old house where I used to sleep over some nights as a kid when Dad was playing with his band. But then the sound changed, a *swoosh-swoosh* woke me from the memory of Christmas Eve at Gran's, waiting up to spot Santa Claus arriving on the front lawn.

It was actually raining. Melbourne's weather was changeable from one minute to the next. No wonder it felt so humid inside the car. Huge droplets of rain went *splat* on the windscreen, round mini-puddles for a second before the wipers chased them away.

Christos was quiet. I was acutely aware of him though, his scent surrounding us in this capsule of a car, his essence teasing my nostrils and urging me closer as we sped through the night towards our destination.

His place. His *bed*.

Was I making a huge mistake? Too soon to say.

But I wanted to take a chance, for the first time in a long time.

I let my gaze drift from the splatting rain drops to the man beside me. His hand taut on the gearstick, tendons in his exposed forearm shifting with the change of gears. Up to his shoulders, broad and muscular under his shirt, to his neck and jaw. So strong. Masculinity in its essential form. His profile was highlighted by the street lights, the straight line of his nose slightly crooked, under close inspection.

I blurted out a question before I could think. "Did you break your nose once?"

Christos turned to me quickly, then looked right back at the road ahead. "Yes. Why do you ask?"

"I noticed your nose is a little crooked. I don't know why I didn't see it before."

"It was a fight back in high school. Stupid kid stuff."

The way he responded, too dismissive, too fast, told me it was anything but. I tangled my fingers together in my lap. I didn't push it. I didn't know why I'd even said anything to break the silence. Besides being completely nervous, verging on completely uncommunicative. Dumbstruck by him and his male beauty.

"We're nearly at my house. I'm at the end of the court, the white house."

"Oh, it's lovely."

It was. And unexpected. A cottage with a small porch out front, lavender along the low picket fence. One tall tree, maybe an oak, stood proud in the garden. It was a proper home, no bachelor pad or flat, not a temporary stop-gap place to lay his head. A few pieces of the puzzle named Christos clicked into place in my mind.

He stared ahead as he spoke in a low tone, hard to hear under the rumble of the engine. But I was all ears. "I'm glad you like it, Lily. I bought it a few years back and I've renovated it from the foundations up. But not to sell. I want to live here for a long time."

I nodded, pressing my lips together. This was a serious man. A keeper, at least potentially. And didn't it make my home fires burn? My belly tightened and my lady parts tingled like they were effervescent.

Who knew responsible home ownership and gardening skills could be such a turn on? I certainly didn't until then.

We pulled up into the paved driveway beside the

cottage. As he put the car into neutral and pulled the hand brake, Christos shrugged, his head lowered. He ran his hands through his hair, as if he didn't know what to do with them. "I can take you home anytime you like. No pressure. But I like you. I want you."

Oh, hubba hubba. Serious and considerate. What a combination.

I leaned across and placed my hand on his arm. The warmth of his skin under my hand was addictive. I wanted more. "I like you too. You know, it could be a case of hero worship. You're a dead-set spunk, Christos Cyriakos."

His laughter shook my fingertips and vibrated through me.

I smiled as I spoke. "Let's go in. Maybe you can give me the grand tour."

Of your bedroom...

Did I say that out loud? No reaction from Christos. Phew. I didn't want him to think I was a raging sex-starved maniac. At least not yet.

Christos opened the car door for me again and I fluttered all over like a beautiful butterfly spreading her wings. This was rather odd, because no man had ever made me feel like a beautiful butterfly.

He held my hand and I exhaled, forcing breath in and out of my lungs. I did not need to pass out. He'd already teased me once about falling at his feet. While I liked a good teasing, I was hoping for foreplay leading to a foregone conclusion.

The rain wasn't as heavy, but a steady pitter-patter hit the paving and sprinkled me in crystalline droplets. It was still warm, still mild. I shook my head to let the rain fall from the loose strands of hair around my face.

Christos raised his right hand and ever-so-gently pushed a tendril of damp hair behind my ear, whispering a touch across my cheekbone. I gasped, the sound muffled by the press of his mouth over mine. But it was over too soon.

I straightened up, shook my head to dislodge the cloudy sex haze, then remembered we were still outside.

We walked hand-in-hand to his front door. He unlocked it with a bunch of keys tinkling in his hand. No other sound awaited us. No rock-star uncles and entourage, no guitars or drum beat. Only the sound of silence. Blissful.

Christos flicked on a couple of lights and the hallway illuminated, gleaming polished oak floorboards and Turkish rugs making a homey first impression. He gestured me to go first through a set of double doors, into the lounge room. Dark wood furniture and a soft-looking suede sofa in light grey awaited.

It was comfortable, clean, organised, but still personal. There was a certificate from the police academy on the mantelpiece above the modern fireplace. A whole wall of photos of smiling dark-haired people dominated the room.

"Do you live all alone?" I waved in the general direction of the photos in their black frames.

Christos smiled in a lopsided way. "Yeah, but I have a large family. Mum and Dad, Grandma. Then there's my three sisters, lots of cousins, nieces and nephews, uncles and aunts. The whole Greek catastrophe."

"Three sisters?"

"Oh, yeah. Two big, one little. They're a handful, but I love them."

"I think it's nice."

I was jealous, to own the truth. Wishing for my own large family one day wasn't being too weird, was it? I only had Uncle Bill and KC left in the whole world. A pang of fierce longing struck me around the middle. I missed KC. Hopefully she'd come and see me soon, once I could afford a plane ticket for her. And I missed Dad, although thinking about him didn't help keep me in the happy, sexytime mood.

"Sit. Relax." Christos sat at one end of his two-seater sofa and I sat at the other end. "Do you want a drink?"

I declined, and sat awkwardly upright. Could I simply shuffle a smidge towards him later? Sooner rather than later. I sat on my hands in case they wandered.

When I chanced a look at Christos, he was fighting off one of his bright smiles. Like he didn't want to admit he knew what I was up to, but possibly he was having similar thoughts. His arm snaked around my shoulders and pulled me towards him, almost with a mind of its own.

"That's better." Christos stroked my shoulder lightly with the tips of his fingers and I swear a tingly sensation hit all sorts of other nerves throughout my body. "Are you feeling better now? You were sad before, when your uncle started playing the Led Zep song."

Ah. He wanted to talk. I squirmed under his gaze, which was heavy on my skin. He was barely touching me, but I felt it. "It was just weird. My dad passed away two years ago and it used to be his band. He played the song all the time when I was a kid."

Christos squeezed my shoulder. "I'm sorry about your father. Was it a long illness?"

"Oh no, it was an accident. He was riding his motorbike, then there was a truck. A collision, you know." My voice was too tight, too strained. I sounded like a woman on the verge of a breakdown. I only hoped it wasn't true. I'd dealt with all this stuff already, hadn't I? I gritted my teeth.

"Shit, sorry. I shouldn't have brought it up." He held me tighter, rubbing his hand up and down my arm. It should have been soothing. But I was nervy.

I couldn't hide the way my hands shook where they now lay on my lap. "He'd been out playing a gig across town. In the morning he wasn't there. I thought he'd got up early for the day job. He was a builder too. But then I got all the messages on my phone."

Christos clenched his jaw tight before he ground out one word. "Police?"

"Yes. Then someone from the hospital asking me to come immediately. I had to wake KC and take her with me. To see Dad. To bring him home. When I got there it was an hour too late."

This time, Christos pulled me against his body so my head rested in the crook of his neck. I breathed him in, all the delicious spicy layers of him.

I closed my eyes for a second or two, willing the nightmare images to fly far away. I didn't need to remember right now.

I sighed. "Is it okay if we don't talk anymore? What I really want, what I need...is more of this." I trailed my index finger up his body from his chest, to his throat, all the way to his mouth. I touched his lips lightly, like I'd asked him to keep a secret.

He shuddered, his breath escaping, brushing my fingers. Lips so surprisingly soft. Raising my head, I kissed a path along the shadow of his jawline, coming to rest on his chin. One more butterfly-like kiss and I pressed my mouth against his.

Then we came together in an almighty crash, like we were on a collision course. His lips pressed down upon mine. The intensity, the taste of him, almost overwhelming. A groan of satisfaction, or frustration, rose from Christos's chest.

My head was spinning, the heady scent of him now surrounding me, amber and cardamom spice teasing me. I opened my lips for him, inviting him to kiss me deeper.

I tilted my head, wrapping my hands around the back of his neck. His tongue met mine. Body pressed flush against the length of mine. I gasped, the feel of him so good, so perfect. My legs parted, dress hiked up almost to my hips as his hand caressed my thigh. His hardness pressed to my softness. A lot of hardness.

What had I been thinking about clothes? Yes. They needed to come off.

I reached for the buttons of Christos's shirt, but I didn't get further than the first one. I didn't want to stop kissing him. Fingers fumbling, I found myself caressing the V of his exposed skin, stroking the thick thatch of chest hair.

One button popped out of its little slot. Only about five to go. I know I moaned into his mouth, because he broke away with a nip on my lower lip. A corresponding tug reached my lower belly, the spot between my thighs, the dull thud of my pulse more insistent.

"Here, let me help." Christos took over unbuttoning, guiding my hands. Then he pressed my palms to the planes of his stomach as the fabric of his shirt fell aside.

"Oooooofff!" I commanded, and Christos answered with a low chuckle.

He leaned back over the arm of his sofa and somehow wrenched himself free from his shirt. Then he was gloriously naked. Half naked. Whatever. I stared, I'm not ashamed to admit it.

The size and scale of Christos, in the flesh, was stupefying. He hadn't seemed so muscular, so built, in a tailored suit, though I knew the strength was there. His olive skin went on for miles, the jet black happy trail of hair becoming finer down the centre of his body, between rows of highly defined abs the likes of which I'd never seen in real life.

"Now, you. Turn around." He used a gravelly voice I'd heard once before. The one which liquified my knickers.

I couldn't help the momentary loss of my faculties. My breath came in shallow pants, making my breasts rise and fall. I knew his eyes were on me, his slow perusal taking in my cleavage, my dress having been pushed down a good way. The outline of my hard nipples was hard to miss, the points pressing against the fabric of my dress. His inspection heated every inch of my skin.

I turned as he'd asked, my back to him, tossing the loose strands of my destroyed hairdo over my right shoulder. I'd started shaking, and my fingers were useless, the zipper at the back of my dress was defeating me. How the hell had I ever got the thing on?

Christos gripped the tag of my zipper, pulling it downwards, slower than I would've expected. Then heat, the soft contact, his lips on my skin. He kissed his way down my spine one vertebra at a time, the muffled *zzzzz* sound of the zip descending, the only sound.

When he came to my waist, he paused and

unhooked my bra, letting his hands wander around my body, cupping my full breasts in his palms over the lace cups. My breath gushed from my lungs. All I could think was: *more.*

A moment later, the fabric of my dress fell from my shoulders, Christos ran his palms over my bare shoulders. My bra straps followed. My back was still facing him. I longed to turn around, but I shied away.

He was quiet. Too quiet.

Not every man appreciated a woman with curves on her bones. What if I wasn't his cup of tea? Not his particular brand of perfume? I pressed my lips together. I had to know.

I twisted my head to the left, glancing over my shoulder. What I saw in Christos's face was not distaste or disinterest. It was blatant hunger. His eyes had darkened and they glittered under the golden lighting overhead. He sat back from me, resting one arm across the back of the sofa. His breathing was harsher, loud now in the quiet room.

Thank God. He wanted me.

"Lily…" He sighed, reaching for me. He took hold of my shoulders and gently urged me to face him. "I knew you'd be beautiful. I just didn't know how stunning."

I let my dress drop down further, the strapless bra following, then inched my arms out of the fabric until it pooled around my waist.

Christos leaned in, then his lips were on me, on my throat, kissing a spot between my clavicles, the indentation there throbbing. I gasped at the intimate contact, the way he pulled me closer to him, holding me firmly by my shoulders. He worked his way down, kissing my chest, the tiny freckles there, down to my breasts.

I watched his movement, his black eyelashes fanning across his cheeks as he lowered his head. I arched my back and gasped with pleasure, as he took one nipple between his lips. He tormented me, sucking my tender flesh into his mouth. He teased my other breast with his fingertips, massaging the underside. He glanced up at me, grinning as he rose up once more, taking my face in his hands.

Our bodies pressed against each other in a long line, Christos on top, me below, stretched out on his sofa. I wrapped my hands around his back and tugged him closer still. And nearly exploded in a ball of flame as his lower body collided with mine. He rocked into me, taking no chance I wouldn't know what he was packing.

Kisses, licking, tasting, biting, his hands on my body, my hands sliding down his back. This was good, so good, but I need more.

His thoughts must have mirrored mine, because he rose up to sit, taking a moment to catch his breath. His left eyebrow arched. "Do you want to stay? We can move to my bedroom."

He was giving me an out clause, if I wanted it. I did not. One thing I knew for sure, I wanted Christos as if my life depended on it.

I whispered, though the words seemed to echo in the pause he'd left. "I want you. I want to stay."

The smile he gifted me made my whole stomach flip, it was so cheeky and self-assured. He had me, and he knew it. His hands were on my breasts, teasing the tips between his fingertips, taunting me until I was a writhing, panting mess.

Only then did he pick me up, one hand under my bottom, the other supporting my back. He. Picked. Me. Up. Then he rose to his feet like I weighed nothing, hoisting me with him in one smooth motion until he was walking, striding really. We were heading for the room at the end of his hallway.

His master bedroom. Where hopefully he would master me.

Hubba hubba.

I kissed his neck, licked it really. He let out a string of muttered expletives. "Bloody hell, Lily, hold on a minute."

I did hold on tight to his neck, clinging on for dear life, but I wasn't going easy on the necking. He was too delicious.

There was clunking and stomping, then I looked up to find Christos staring straight ahead at the king-sized bed. It was covered in a downy beige quilt and some dark blue cushions with little birds on them. For something so apparently comfortable, the bed suddenly loomed large and intimidating.

I didn't want to ruin the moment by being nervous. He wouldn't reject me. He wasn't my ex.

But I didn't have to worry, because Christos lowered me onto the edge of the bed, then dropped to his knees before me. He inched the remains of my dress down over my hips, or rather peeled me like a banana out of its skin.

I wiggled to give him access, and his hands followed the contours of my ample bottom and thighs. If I was self-conscious about my top half, revealing my bottom half gave me pause.

True, I was wearing my sure-fire, confidence-building black silky knickers with peek-a-boo lacy bits. But it was the dimply, less than slender bits of me I was afraid he wouldn't find appealing.

I needn't have worried. As I kicked my dress off from one ankle, leaving my shoes on, he made a very gratifying noise. Somewhere between a sigh and a groan, it hit me right between the thighs.

"Lily... Damn, I forgot what I was going to say." He rubbed his hands over his face, then his gaze connected with mine.

His eyes so deep, so fathomless, I knew I'd get lost in them forever. If I wasn't careful.

He reached for the drawer of the low bedside table. Rustling around, he pulled a foil packet from inside. Wordless, he kept his hot gaze on me, making me melt further into the bed, jelly-legged as I was.

With a clack of a belt buckle and a super-fast unzipping, his pants were history. Shoes kicked off. Gone. Christos was naked before me as he sheathed himself. He was hard and ready. I swallowed on a parched throat.

I let my gaze roam over his body, drinking him in. I wouldn't be exaggerating if I said choirs of angels sang and demigods wept at the sight. Not much. I bit my lower lip to stop myself taking a bite out of him.

I shimmied back onto the bed, pulling the covers down as I went. I patted the spot beside me on the smooth white sheets.

He joined me, rolling me into the middle of the bed. I shivered as he raised himself up on his elbows above me, lower body pinning me down.

Pinning was good. Pinning was winning.

I raised my legs and wrapped them tight around Christos's back, as he pressed against me, just there, just right. When he finally entered me, he covered my mouth with his, kissing me, smothering the gasp. It shot out of my mouth a second later as he angled his hips. *Almost.* Then he pressed into me fully…

Oh, hello. Right. There.

I broke our kiss and cried out.

"Holy moly chocolate gumdrops! Christos!" Because really, intelligent word choices are overrated at such a moment.

His shoulders shook with suppressed laughter as he pressed into my body again, his dark chuckle a delight as he took me.

Took me, took me, took me, oh...

I squeezed my legs tighter around the small of his back, rocking my hips.

He kissed down the side of my throat, mumbling sweet nothings all the while. Well, mostly nothings. I think I heard the words, 'so sexy', along with dirtier words. Which fired me up like nobody's business.

My hands made their merry way from his shoulders, down the smooth line of his back, to grip his mighty fine butt. I double-checked it was mighty fine, enjoying the contours beneath my palms. I pulled him closer and Christos responded, angling his hips just so.

I let out a cry of surprise, or shock. A sudden rush of electric joy zapped through all the billions of nerves in my body. My body shuddered, then tensed. The gorgeous man above me tensed too, leaning down to kiss my mouth as I shook with wave after wave of pleasure. Until I was spent. Wrecked. Wrung out.

His movements sped, Christos raised my hips with both his hands, taking me deeper than ever. His ragged shout, my name, was pure joy, as he tensed and then fell in a heap on top of me. A hot, heavy and gorgeous-smelling heap.

I didn't even mind his weight on my body. We pressed together in all the best places, and his head rested beside mine on one plush pillow. I snuggled against him.

Christos kissed the delicate spot below my ear and

whispered, "You killed me. Lily, you bloody killed me. Mmmm."

I shivered, because the way he was kissing my ear lobe was divine. But he was generally yummy. Possibly addictive.

"I hope I didn't kill you, because I'll be needing more. More kissing." I pressed my lips to his cheek. "More touching." I let my hands drift south, below the belt, so to speak.

Christos grumbled, "I have to get up. Give me ten minutes and I'm all yours again."

"Ten minutes? Impressive." My cheek muscles tugged into a wide grin, and I rolled to my side as he climbed off me.

Watching his muscles shift as he walked away was something to write sonnets about.

Christos entered the bathroom adjoining his bedroom and shut the door. I stretched out my limbs like a contented cat, then pulled the quilt up to my chin.

This was what I needed. Christos. A whole lot of loving and a long, dreamy sleep.

CHAPTER 10

"What?" I asked groggily. I rolled onto my back as the hunka hunka burning love beside me shifted. It was dark. Still the middle of the night.

Christos shushed me, leaning towards the table on his side of the bed.

I blinked my eyes half open and rubbed them with the backs of my hands. The room was pitch black. A yellowish glow, a lamp turned on.

Did he want me again? Mmmm. I hoped so. He'd already proven himself multitalented in the last few hours.

I glanced across at him. He was out of bed, holding his phone, staring at the screen. In the glow from the phone's screen his face was illuminated, the lines of consternation emphasised. He wore boxer shorts, but reached for his trousers slung over a nearby chair.

Getting dressed? What? Why?

I sat up as far as I could, leaning on my elbows. I wasn't awake enough for being upright.

Christos had his trousers half on, phone pressed to his ear, held in place with his shoulder. He zipped up his pants as he mumbled. "What time?" There was a pause, then he spoke again. "No, it's okay. I'm on my way."

I rubbed my eyes again and spoke through a croaky throat. "Christos?"

"It's just work. Go back to sleep."

I scrunched up my face, then yawned. "But the store's not even open. It's the middle of the night."

He sighed, shrugging into a fresh shirt he'd grabbed from the wardrobe behind him. "My other job. I haven't had a chance to tell you. Don't worry, I'll be back soon."

I brushed my loose hair behind my ear. "Do you want me to go home? I could call a taxi?"

He shook his head, then leaned over and placed a gentle kiss on my lips. "No way. Sleep. I'll be back."

I'll be back. Famous last words.

He wasn't back. It was 5.53 am according to the clock on the lonely side of Christos's vast bed. It had been over an hour already.

This was weird. Why would he leave me alone in his house? In his bed? I wasn't complaining about being in his bed, but I was pretty sure he was supposed to be in it too.

And what was this other job? He hadn't mentioned it before. I didn't like it. It smacked of lies and deception.

I did not want to get involved with a liar. Or get *more* involved. Because I was involved with Christos up to my eyeballs. I could still feel the imprint of his kisses on my swollen lips, the press of him against my body, especially in certain areas. I rubbed my hands up and down my own arms, trying to chase away the scatter of goosebumps creeping over my skin.

Should I stay in bed and wait for Christos? He'd asked me to stay put, but now I was awake I didn't want to lie still. An urgent trip to the bathroom was in order anyway. I dragged myself out of the bed, kicking the bedding away.

Once I'd been to the bathroom and took care of business, I treated myself to a quick but gloriously hot shower with the fresh green/citrus soap, the scent of Christos's pillow. Then I ran a comb through my mess of damp, wavy hair. I returned to the bedroom and looked around blankly. I didn't want to wear my crumpled red dress from last night. Apart from looking the worse for wear, it was an alarming shade of red for so early in the day.

Instead, I crossed the room to Christos's wardrobe and flicked through hangers of shirts, folded trousers, jackets, and a uniform I'd never seen before.

I lifted the hanger from the rail. It was a police officer's navy blue uniform. He'd be incredibly sexy in it. Maybe I'd ask him to model it for me some time, and let him order me around.

But I thought Christos would have given his uniform back once he'd quit the force. Strange. I put it back on the rail, then found a plain sky blue t-shirt to wear. I popped it over my head and smoothed it down my body. It was huge, long enough to hit mid-thigh. Roomy enough to be comfortable.

Unsure of what to do, I wandered into the lounge room in search of my handbag and phone, last seen on the coffee table. I sat on the squishy sofa, and the rush of memories of Christos and I last night hit me. This is where he'd undressed me. Kissed me.

I grabbed my bag and searched through it, until I found my phone. I sank into the sofa cushions and checked my messages.

Notifications flashed at me. There was a text from KC She was coming to Melbourne to see me...today. Since when? But she'd sent a flight number and was obviously already on her way. I pressed a hand to my temple. My head had started throbbing.

She could have told me she was coming. She called me a mother hen, said I worried too much. It was true. I'd stepped into the role of surrogate parent early on. Since our mother passed away when KC was only a baby, I was the one she looked up to. Then Dad died two years ago and it was all on me. Now KC was grown up, she had to find her feet. I'd helped get her through high school at least.

I tapped out a quick text asking her to please call me as soon as she landed in Melbourne. I'd probably be at work, away from my phone, but I'd call her back as soon as I could.

The other message was from Christos, sent ten minutes ago:

On my way home. I'm bringing coffee and croissants. Please be there... Miss you already.

Oh, he was sweet. Sweet but mysterious.

A resounding *click* had me sitting up straighter, crossing my legs. A jangle of keys followed, then Christos opened the front door. A shaft of blue-ish early morning light filtered in behind him like a spotlight, streaming into the hallway.

I pressed my lips together to keep from shouting at him, or more likely, telling him never to leave me again. Which wouldn't be good.

He pushed in through the door, balancing a bag of sweet-smelling somethings and two paper coffee cups all in one hand.

"Hi there." He stopped short. "Oh, forget it. I don't want to act all cool and casual. I'm just going to kiss the hell out of you, all right?"

I nodded mutely as he crossed the room in three strides and dumped the food on the coffee table.

He sat beside me, wrapping his arms around my waist and pulling me close. He tilted his head and nudged my nose with his, then pressed his lips to mine. This kiss was sweeter, softer than the ones last night. I sucked in a gasp when he ran the tip of his tongue across my lower lip. Random tingles went flying all over the joint. I think my knees melted.

He mumbled against my mouth. "I love you in my shirt."

My heart thudded wildly at his choice of the word *love*, though I knew it was only sexy-talk. I opened to him, teasing my tongue against his, shifting my body towards his at the same time. My body heated, growing hungry for more.

One of Christos's hands was on my thigh now, inching its way up beneath the hem of the t-shirt I wore. I grabbed his hand and stopped it in its tracks. I leaned back and stared at him. Before we went any further, I needed answers.

"Where did you go? Why did you slink out like a criminal? Not cool. Or polite. Especially considering I was still stupid with post-orgasm glow."

"Were you really?" he chuckled, so I narrowed my eyes and glared until he stopped. "Okay. Let me explain."

"Yes, please."

He sighed and sat back against the arm of the sofa. "I wanted to tell you, but not at work. I was going to tell you last night, but then you distracted me. It's confidential. This needs to stay between us."

"Okay."

Christos ran his hand across his jaw, the raspy sound of friction against unshaven whiskers evoking memories of last night. But this was no time for me to be distracted.

"I didn't resign from the police force. I'm working undercover as a security guard, investigating a ring of thieves suspected to be connected to the store. Organised crime, to be blunt."

I blinked a few times. Christos was still a cop? So he *was* a liar. A practised and professional one. "You mean you've been lying to me. We slept together and I don't even know who you are."

I crossed my arms tight around my waist, hugging myself. This wasn't the way things were meant to go. He was supposed to take me back to bed for sexytimes and take me out to dinner sometime.

Christos frowned, the wrinkles formed on his forehead aging him several years before my eyes. He was stressed-out, and I hadn't noticed. I should have, but then he'd been busy lying. "I couldn't explain before. Stock has gone missing from the cosmetics department. Thousands of dollars' worth. There was an attempted break-in to the main storeroom. But our major concern has been cash siphoned from the registers. I'm sorry to ask you this now, and I hope I haven't stuffed up things between us. Have you noticed anything unusual, Lily?"

This was what he'd asked me to help him with earlier on. I wracked my brain, and an image popped into my head. "Now I think about it, yes. I did see something strange. A staff member dressed all in black, someone I didn't recognise, at the back of the store-room. They had a whole pallet loaded with perfume, but it didn't make it out to the floor. I'd forgotten all about it."

I sat up straighter, watching Christos's expression change. The frown was replaced by a raised eyebrow. "What day was it? Think carefully."

Looking up at the ceiling to concentrate, something pinged. "Tuesday. I remember now, because I was planning to go to the movies after work with Petula. Cheapskate Tuesday, you know."

He nodded. "What did the person in the storeroom look like? Can you describe them?"

I bit my lip. Christos glanced down at my mouth for a moment, before meeting my eyes again. "It was dark —darker than usual. I went inside to get a couple of boxes of perfume. Our most popular spring fragrance. I headed to the Fine Fragrances section and noticed one of the flouro lights was out. The person was at the end of the aisle, a few metres away. I think it was a young man but I can't be sure. Skinny, wearing a black shirt and jeans. And a black cap."

I blinked and opened my eyes a little wider. The whole thing was odd, once I said it out loud. We don't wear caps at work, unless it's for a special product promotion. I couldn't remember seeing anyone wearing one recently, apart from this person.

"Good. Very helpful. I'll get you to speak to my colleague, Jason. Tell him what you told me. I knew you weren't involved."

I blinked again, but this time in shock. "You thought I was involved? One of the criminals?"

He put his hand out towards me, as if he wanted to take my hand, but I inched away from him.

He sighed. "No. I didn't think you were involved, but I couldn't prove it. My superiors asked me investigate you. You're a new staff member. The incidents ramped up over the last few weeks. The security cameras were deactivated in the storeroom last Tuesday, about the same time you went in. Jason thought it was you but I told him he was wrong."

I took a deep breath. I could have told him to go to hell, since the lying and the suspecting me of stealing wasn't a ringing endorsement of Christos as boyfriend material. But as I breathed through a red haze behind my eyes, my flare of anger faded to mild mauve. I understood. He was supposed to investigate, and he was. I just didn't want him lying or spying on me.

I sat up straight, then smoothed my hair behind my shoulders. I was as together as I was going to get, pre-coffee. I glanced at the coffees sitting on the nearby table and grabbed one. I took a sip, savouring the bitter-sweet flavour filling my mouth, a hint of vanilla. I rested the cup on my knee.

When I spoke, I was dead serious. Even I was surprised by the gravel in my tone. "I want you to be completely honest with me from now on. If we can't talk at work, we'll talk afterwards. Otherwise we're history, okay?"

"Okay, that's fair. Thanks, Lily."

He reached for the other coffee and opened the bag of pastries. We devoured our breakfast in silence, because mind-bending revelations aside, a person had to eat. I'm glad Christos understood the importance of good food.

Christos loaned me some of his sweat pants to wear on the drive back to my place. We only said a few words in the car about the song on the radio, *Fall At Your Feet* by Crowded House. We both loved it. When he kissed me goodbye outside my house it was a chaste peck on the cheek. Hardly the ending I'd been expecting after the night we'd shared.

But life is never what you'd been expecting. It's an unexpected collision with a truck, a dead father, getting kicked out of your family home with a stack of debts and a sixteen-year-old sister to finish raising. It's being twenty-five years old but feeling one hundred and five.

I walked into my house, finding the debris of Bill's party still decorating the living room. And a couple of random people asleep on the sofa.

I marched straight into my bedroom and shut the door on all the mess. I had to get ready for work.

CHAPTER 11

W ork, work, work.
I stood behind the perfume counter,
wrapping presents with shaking fingers. And aching
feet. I kicked off each shoe and rolled my ankles, one at
a time. I'd wrapped twenty presents so far. About fifty
to go. I'd get the other staff to help later.

Giselle was serving our only customer. She chatted
as she applied scented body lotion to the older
woman's hands. "*Oui*, I am French, but I do love
Australie. My mother and father came here when I was
in high school. They worked for a French cosmetics
company. So it is in my blood!"

Giselle demonstrated the finer points of fragrance
layering—showing the customer how to use multiple
products to extend the life of a fragrance on the skin.

I stood in my stocking-clad feet for a few seconds
before sliding my shoes back on and submitting to the

slow torture again. I'd only been at work for a couple of hours, but the wrong shoes were turning me into a grumpy cow. Well, grumpier.

What could you expect of a day beginning with lies and suspicion? I was now watching every single one of my colleagues with new eyes, clouded by mistrust. I stopped wrapping, scissors still in hand, turning left and right, checking out the activity on the floor. Everything was quiet.

Petula was across the aisle, leaning against the manicure bar. She was sorting new nail polishes into an attractive rainbow colour wheel display. She'd started work here around the same time as me. Could she be a criminal?

What about Giselle? I doubted it, since she'd been working here a couple of years. But what if she'd been corrupted by someone?

Then there were casual spritzer chicks who I hardly knew. A bunch of casual staff had just started in the fashion department, as well as upstairs in what I called The Land of Christmas. The decorations and toys took over most of the fourth floor at this time of year and a team of sales staff were brought in for the season. Plus the Home Entertainment guys. I hated to think it, but some of them looked dodgy.

Is this what it would be like to be married to a cop? Worried, suspicious of everyone?

The thought could get out of my head. It didn't

belong in my mixed-up brain at all. I put down the scissors and took several slow breaths.

I'd barely started seeing Christos. He'd met my peculiar uncle, which probably counted as meeting my family, it was true. I'd slept with him, oh yes. But *marriage*? I was getting way ahead of myself. I was in danger of becoming an obsessive basket case. And it wasn't even lunchtime.

Christos appeared, as if he'd materialised out of thin air. He marched straight down the centre aisle of the cosmetics department. His posture was stiff and waves of invisible furiousness rolled off him. Maybe not everyone could tell, but it was obvious to me.

His jaw was hard, his expression carefully neutral, but his eyes were flinty. He scanned the floor, looking around the area near the escalators. He stopped, hands linked behind his back.

I guessed he was looking for something, or some*one*. A customer approached the counter and I smiled, as Christos turned his full focus on me. He was metres away, but a slow, knowing smile spread over his face, his eyes sparkling with fallen stars under the overhead Christmas lights. That look was all mine and I soaked it up like a sponge.

I swallowed on a dry throat as flashes of sense-memory from last night overtook my mind and body. His lips against the soft skin of my stomach, the flutter of his breath, travelling downwards...

Giselle approached my side and promptly nudged me, hard. Right in the ribs.

"Oooof!" I gasped.

"Wake up, Ms Lily. We have real-life customers waiting." Giselle's voice floated down to me, from some faraway place back on planet earth.

When I glanced at her, Giselle was wearing her trademark bemused French woman expression. It was rather like resting bitch face, but more sophisticated.

I shook my head, hormones rattling randomly. I shot a last glance at Christos as he marched off towards the staff area at the other end of the floor. I served my customer with the standard level of service, an extra huge grin tugging at my cheeks. I couldn't seem to turn it off now.

Giselle sidled up to me again by the cash register as I rang up a beautiful bottle of imported Italian eau de toilette with matching shower gel in a heart-shaped box. I studied the box as I placed it in a shopping bag with the customer's receipt, ignoring Giselle as long as possible.

Finally Giselle stamped her stiletto heel and demanded, "Well?"

I raised my left eyebrow and pretended innocence. My strained giggle might have given me away though. "Well, what?"

Giselle sighed. "Did you *passer a la casserole* with the handsome Mr Security?"

"Make a casserole? No, we did not. We did share

croissants this morning though, so I think you'd approve." My cheeks stretched into another grin and my face heated.

"Oh, I approve. Mmm-hmm." Giselle fist-bumped me in a most un-Giselle-like way.

I turned back to the floor to see a determined Petula speed-walking in my direction. She skidded to a halt right in front of the teetering tower of gift-wrapped fake presents. My eyes widened. I watched to see whether they'd topple.

I reached for the top of the pile and Petula slapped her hand over mine, squeezing my fingers. "Psst, tell me. Tell. Me!"

My new friend was aggressive as a pit bull over a titbit of gossip. Okay, it was more than a titbit. I'd been well and truly laid after a drought of almost two years. It was certainly newsworthy. Especially on the cosmetics floor, where admiring the finer specimens among the male staff was a favourite spectator sport.

"Me, Christos, breakfast this morning. You can join the dots." I leaned closer to her, lowering my voice. "He crossed all the Ts and dotted the Is too, if you catch my drift." I nodded meaningfully.

Petula removed her hand from mine and pressed it over her own mouth, to muffle her squeal. It leaked out anyway. "I knew he was meant for you. He gave you the man-in-lust eyes from day one. I knew it!" She gestured to her wrist, then mouthed, "Lunch, one o'clock."

I agreed to lunch and Petula sauntered back to her counter. I pressed my lips together to keep from bursting out laughing. It took me a minute to recognise the bubbly, frothy feeling in my belly, the light-headed excitement overtaking my whole body.

It was probably silly. It was undeniably hopeful. It was happiness. Grumpy cow mood deactivated.

E *mergency, emergency...*

So much for a gossipy lunch with Petula. At five minutes to one, the wailing alarm and the recorded emergency voice sounded and we all looked around with startled kangaroo-in-headlights faces. This wasn't a fire drill, this was real.

I signalled to my team to follow me. Giselle and Gillian, who had just arrived, lined up behind me. We had to exit the cosmetics area and head towards the emergency exit through the main double doors. I checked on two casual staff who were rostered on as perfume spritzers near the main entrance. They knew to evacuate.

Christos and his offsider, Jason, a younger, sandy-haired, chubby-faced man with ill-fitting jacket and trousers, were ushering people through the main doors. They were talking to two staff with fetching yellow Fire Warden helmets.

Our area warden was the scary floor manager, Hyacinth. I saw her lurking by the door. She spoke into a mobile phone and stood with one hand on her hip.

The automated voice on the overhead public address system did little to calm people's panic. The whole store was being evacuated, everyone exiting right out into the street. Customers went where we directed them.

Something was going down, and it wasn't good. Likely a bomb threat.

I wouldn't panic. It was probably just kids messing around, getting a thrill out of setting off the alarm. Unless…

What if it was the criminals Christos was investigating? What if something real was going down, right here, right now? I should have been scared, but a strange thrill snaked its way down my spine.

I cast a glance over my shoulder as I exited the main doors. Christos was in the middle of a powwow with three yellow hats. He towered above them all, and his eyes connected with mine. The expression on his face softened, melted like butter on the top of a pancake. I only held his gaze for a second but I pressed my hand to my chest to keep my heart in place.

I swooshed out the door, carried forward by Giselle and Petula and a bunch of girls from the make-up-artist crew. I spotted a customer with one eye made-up with heavy winged eyeliner and one eye still nude.

The cool air-conditioning evaporated instantly as I stepped outside, and the sun's rays pounded against my exposed face and arms. It had to be over thirty degrees outside. I was pasty, being a redhead, and I needed a hat or I'd burn in no time. The shade of a spindly gum tree planted next to the pavement would have to do. Petula was on my heels.

"Do you think we'll have to go back to work today? I could really use an afternoon off. Maybe I'll go to the beach." Petula sounded wistful, her head tilted upwards at the cloudless blue sky.

I shaded my eyes with my right hand. "I'd either be sunburned lobster red or I'd get heatstroke. If we get the afternoon off, I'm going home to my air-con and putting my feet up. Maybe I'll watch a movie. Have a glass of white wine or two."

Petula tossed her hair over one shoulder and sighed. "No hot security guard to keep you warm if the air-conditioning gets too breezy?"

"I might invite him over to rub my feet. He's good with his hands." I let the comment hang there for a few seconds, until we both descended into fits of giggles. Honestly, we were both mature adults.

A few metres away, our elusive store manager, Mr Harrison, made an appearance. His grey hair glowed in the sunlight. He stood on a low concrete wall and spoke through a megaphone. "Please follow instructions from fire wardens and the fire department. Move to your nearest emergency assembly point. There's a potential gas leak and we need everyone to stay back from the building."

I spotted the red whoosh of a fire truck coming down the main driveway, the *nee-naw* of the siren blaring. It followed the road alongside the shopping centre, turning into the parking area nearest the main doors of the department store. A team of fire fighters headed inside the building. We couldn't see anything else from our spot outside.

I chatted to Petula to pass the time. She was thinking of inviting Kurt to her family's Christmas dinner. This was clearly a big step, so I didn't press for too much information, since she had a pinched look around her eyes. Petula needed to go and buy Christmas presents, so she wandered off.

Half an hour later, most of the customers had gone and there was only a handful of us still standing around waiting. A lot of staff had gone for lunch, with or without permission. Who knew where Giselle had disappeared to?

I gasped when someone snuck up behind me and whispered in my ear. Someone tall, with a familiar scent. Heat flushed from my chest and neck all the way to my face. "Lily, you should go home."

I spun around on my heels and faced Christos and started, my mouth hanging open. He'd stripped off his jacket down to his white business shirt. And he was wet. The cotton fabric of his shirt was semi-sheer and stuck to his chest and stomach in a lickable way.

Christos tilted his head to one side. "We're closing the store for the rest of the day since the sprinkler system went off in the offices and everything's wet. But I have to work." He ran his hand through his hair, slicked back with water.

I must have pouted. Christos's gaze dropped to my mouth. He mumbled under his breath, something like *'dammit'* and *'later'*. I distinctly heard the words, *'that sexy mouth'*.

A warm ribbon of velvety desire unfurled deep inside me. I wanted to wrap him up in ribbons and never let him escape.

He took a step back from me and shook his head. "I'd better get back."

"I understand." I did, even though he didn't tell me the whole story. Something was going on, beyond a gas leak. Something required his urgent attention, since he took off at a jog.

I hesitated, shifting my weight from one foot to the other. My phone was inside, in my locker. I needed it, since I expected KC to call. She'd be arriving soon and I wasn't even prepared. This whole week had been one unusual thing after another. I didn't know which way was up.

But I was more preoccupied about Christos maybe calling me later than where my own sister was. How bizarre.

A young woman with curly blonde hair was outside now, handing out bottled water and telling staff to go home. She approached me with water in her outstretched hand, and a gap-toothed smile. She reminded me of my sister.

"I'm Bron from HR. You should collect your personal items and leave for today. The store's closing." She spoke to a few of us still milling around. I couldn't see any of my team though.

I accepted the water with thanks, then entered the staff door and made my way to the locker area. I couldn't wait to get home.

How would the night unfurl? Would Christos call me and come over? Would I be able to introduce him to KC and get her opinion on my spunk of a date? Maybe we could all spend Christmas together.

I couldn't wait. I had a skip in my step as I walked home.

CHAPTER 12

❄

I don't know why I'd been so excited. Nothing ever worked out the way I thought it would.

I walked into the house to find it emptier, quieter than usual. There was no music playing, no noise at all. All the beer bottles and general mess from last night's band party had been cleaned up. Things were missing from the bookshelf, and the kitchen table. There was no sign of my uncle.

All signs pointed in one direction. Bill had left, without warning. I thought he'd planned to stay until the new year.

I wandered through the house, looking for signs of life. Nothing. His clothes were gone, most of his instruments. I shuffled into the kitchen, feeling more than a little lost.

Then I saw the envelope. A note on the kitchen counter. He was already on his way to LA. He took off earlier than expected because he'd be playing at a music industry shindig on New Year's Eve.

Bill had given his new address in the US and left me two sets of keys to this house. I gasped when I pulled something else out of the envelope. A bundle of cash in a rubber band. I flicked through it. Five hundred dollars. I let out a slow breath from between my teeth. What a relief. He'd used enough electricity last night alone to send me broke.

Thank you, Bill. I was grateful. He'd really helped by offering me a place to live.

I'd have to call him and thank him properly, once he'd settled in.

I wandered around the quiet house for a while, then showered. I found myself with nothing to do and no one to talk to, with three days to go until Christmas. How sad.

Home delivered pizza, popcorn and wine substituted for a healthy dinner, which was fine and dandy. I settled into the sofa in my floral kimono, air-con at full blast and *Die Hard* on TV. It was the perfect Christmas movie, since 80s Bruce Willis ignored all the seasonal shenanigans to blow-up the baddies, all while focusing like a true hero on getting home to his wife. For some strange reason, this time I was tearing up as I watched it.

And Christos? I tried calling him, I tried texting. I thought about catching a taxi to his house to surprise him. But I didn't have the confidence in our new *thing* to arrive at his place looking to stay over.

KC took her sweet time too. She texted at ten o'clock to say she as on her way. It was nearly midnight before I heard a car pull into the driveway. I was sitting up waiting for her but pretended I wasn't.

I'd only just given in to my mood and downloaded *When Harry Met Sally*, because I was a sappy fool. I wanted to watch the New Year's Eve scene at the end when Harry finally declares his love for Sally, happy-ever-after style. But it wasn't fair, because I wasn't having what she was having.

My sister rang the doorbell and I got off my behind, taking time to stretch out my spine. I strolled to the door, casual as could be. No need to let on I'd been worried about her. When I checked through the spy hole in the front door, it was definitely KC.

It was also definitely Christos standing right behind her, towering above her head. I flung the door open, held my kimono closed at the front and let out a strangled shriek.

"What the hell took you so long to get here? Are you trying to give me a heart attack?" I didn't know which one of them I was yelling at, but I flung my arms around my sister and pulled her close.

Christos stood with his head half in shadow, the porch light giving off a dim golden glow. He had his hands stuffed in his pockets, a serious yet confused look on his face. I couldn't help feeling worried.

Worried about him. This was new. My family were the people I worried about, not boyfriends.

I dragged KC inside the hallway by her shoulders. "Where have you been?"

She ducked her head so her honey-blond hair fell around her face. "I had business here this afternoon."

Business? She was eighteen years old, just out of school and as far as I knew had never uttered the word *business* before in her life. She was an artsy-fartsy type, like Dad and Bill.

"What are you talking about?" She didn't reply.

I flicked my head from KC to Christos, who was hovering on my doorstep. I pulled him forward by the front of his shirt. "Come in. Christos, meet my sister, Katherine. Everyone calls her KC. Sister, meet Christos. My..."

I was struck dumb. Brain boggled. What was Christos to me? We hadn't discussed it.

He stepped forward and extended his hand to my sister. "I'm her friend. From work. It's a pleasure to meet you."

KC looked up at me, raised both eyebrows and then shook Christos's hand. "Hello, Christos-friend-from-work." My sister turned her head towards me and mouthed the word 'sexy' at me. She reminded me so much of Bill, all I could do was stare.

My attention landed on three enormous suitcases on the front path. For a wild moment I thought Christos was moving in with me. But no, of course not.

I pointed to the luggage outside, then wagged my finger at KC "What's all this? You've got some explaining to do, missy."

KC groaned and stepped towards me. "I wanted to surprise you."

I opened my mouth to yell and she interrupted, seamlessly. "I know you don't like surprises, but this one is good. I'm moving to Melbourne too. I got into the college of the arts."

The college of the arts? In Melbourne? I didn't even know she'd applied there. I stumbled back a good few steps and put my hands on my hips. "What? When? What are you talking about?"

Over KC's head, I saw Christos move. Quietly, efficiently, he pulled the suitcases inside the front door. He stepped inside again, but seemed at a loss for what to do with himself. He leaned against the wall and put his hands in his jeans pockets.

KC turned to him and smiled in her shy way, then she briefly caught my eyes. "I didn't tell you I'd applied because I knew how worried you were about money. And other stuff." She raised her head and met my stare this time.

Something defiant was lurking there behind her blue eyes. "I broke up with Johnno so you don't have to worry about him. I want to live here with you and go to uni. I'll get a job, too. I can wait tables or something."

I had no words. They were lodged somewhere in the back of my throat. My girl was growing up after all.

I extended my arms and she fell into my hug, letting me wrap her in my arms. She hadn't let me hug her for over a year. Not since our massive fight over her awful boyfriend. After a moment, I whispered, "What are you studying?"

She beamed at me then. "I had the panel interview today for the Fine Arts degree. I want to study photography."

I grinned, kissing the top of her head. Her hair smelled like sunshine. "Fantastic! Better than fantastic. It's sublime. Isn't that an artistic word?"

KC laughed, her eyes twinkling as she pulled away. "It's totally arty. I'll put my things in Bill's room. He said I could."

I tilted my head to one side. A couple of things fell into place. Bill's sudden departure might not have been so unplanned after all. "When did you speak to him?"

My sister shrugged. "Last weekend. I told him I wasn't sure if I'd got into the college yet, but he said I should stay with you anyway. He said you missed me."

I sniffed, since my nose had apparently started dripping. Not to mention my eyes. I wiped them with the back of my hand. Then Christos was there, wrapping his arm around my shoulders.

KC laughed again, a sound I was thankful to hear. She'd gone off the rails in the last couple of years, especially in the first year after Dad died. But now maybe she was back on track.

"I'll leave you and your *boyfriend* to chat." With a last

waggle of her pierced eyebrow, KC walked off, dragging one of her cases behind her. She looked so grown-up suddenly, wiggling away in her black dress.

I gaped after her. Christos rubbed his hand up and down my back in a soothing yet tingly way. I was confused. Also grateful. And aroused.

"Come and sit down." Christos took my hand and directed me to my own sofa. I went willingly. Maybe he'd kiss me soon.

He sat down next to me, but left a sizeable gap between us. "I'm glad your sister's here. I want you to be happy, Lily."

Why did he sound so ominous? "What's going on?"

"I need you to trust me."

Alarm bells were clanging in my head now. "Trust you, in what way? To remember my birthday and give me orgasms?"

"I don't even know your birthday yet," he deadpanned. Seriously, his face was as expressionless as a frying pan. I certainly wanted to throw an egg at it.

"Fourth of June. But that's not the point."

"Right. It's the work situation. I'm not allowed to see anyone personally who might be involved in a case. My supervisor had words with me."

I crossed my arms over my belly. "He had words with you? About me?"

"Yes. I told him I'd been with you the other night. Let's say he was less than impressed with my 'conduct' during an investigation."

I narrowed my eyes. *Hell, no.* Christos was not dumping me because some old police chief or secret undercover security dude told him to. I was not having it.

I shook my head. "No. I don't care what he says. You're not breaking up with me. I won't allow it." I might have used my take-no-prisoners, quasi-mum voice on him, like I would with KC.

His chuckle was low and naughty. "I like you bossy. But I'm not going to break up with you." He reached for my face and brushed his thumb over my lips. "I can't give you up. We just need to lay low for a while."

"Lay low? What does this entail exactly? Are you allowed to," I coughed, glancing down the hall, lowering my voice on account of my sister, "sleep over?"

"No. Not if I follow the rule book to the letter. But undercover officers have a certain latitude, especially if they have to make decisions on the spot, or keep a witness on side."

My mood brightened with the implications. A witness. Me. "Are you saying you have to pretend to seduce me to keep me as a happy witness?" I moved a little closer to him, tucking my legs up under me on the sofa.

Christos watched me closely, my bare legs in particular. His hand moved to the nape of my neck, running his fingers through my loose hair. "I have to pretend what we have is pretence. Only for a while."

He'd lost me, with all the pretending talk. He wasn't pretending to stroke the sensitive spot on the side of my throat. He didn't pretend to lean over and press his mouth to mine.

Christos kissed my lips like his life hung in the balance, like he may never have another chance. I clung to his shoulders and held on tight.

He pulled away suddenly, breathing hard. "We have to keep this quiet at work, okay? For now. Once the investigation's over, I'll be out of the store and we can be together."

"Hold on." I raised my right hand in a stop-sign signal. There was a whole lot of information in those sentences. "You're leaving the store?"

Of course I realised how silly I sounded as soon as I spoke. He was a cop, not a department store security guard. Real life would come knocking soon.

At least Christos didn't make me feel silly. He pressed his forehead against mine. "I'll be onto a new case soon, if we catch these guys. I might not be able to tell you what I'm working on. Not straight away."

I sighed and pushed my hair behind my ears. "Okay. I get it. But will you stay with me tonight?" My voice was breathier than I'd intended.

Christos tightened his jaw until it clicked. "I'm sorry, I can't. The team's waiting for me."

"Come into the bedroom. I'll let you interrogate me," I teased. I rose from the sofa and walked towards my room, putting a little extra sway in my step.

His low groan was music to my ears. He followed me into the hallway, but stopped short of my bedroom door. I stood in the doorway twirling the long belt of my robe. He had to know I was naked under the satiny fabric.

But my last-minute seduction attempt didn't work. He backed away from me and blustered out the words, "I really have to go. Sorry."

He kissed me on the cheek and was out the front door before I could even say goodnight.

CHAPTER 13

❄

CHRISTMAS EVE-EVE

Next morning, I grinned at my sister across the breakfast table, as shimmery summer light streamed in through the Venetian blinds and fell on the pine table. It was so good to have KC staying with me. No, she wasn't just staying with me, she was living with me again.

I sipped my mug of coffee and she ate toast with Vegemite while she told me about her university course. "I think it's going to be amazing. Some top artists and performers are college alumni. I'll have to work hard on my portfolio. And I've already got a huge reading list of photography and art books for the summer."

She was glowing. My little sister was excited and

ready for this new challenge in her life. I couldn't have been happier for her.

KC suddenly sat bolt upright, her eyes wide. "Oh, I forgot. A letter came for you. I had the mail held at the post office when I went to stay at the Martins' house and I didn't get it right away." She dashed off to the living room and came back with her large handbag.

KC had been staying with her best friend Melanie Martin's family for the past couple of months. Deidre Martin, Melanie's mum, made sure KC was okay. Deidre was a supremely capable lawyer in her early 50s and a wonderful mother-figure. I was almost jealous of how Deidre treated KC like part of her family.

Now my sister was back at the table, rummaging through her bag. She pulled out a large envelope and handed it to me. "I don't know what's inside but it looks official. I didn't open it."

It did look official, scarily so. The name of a law firm was printed on the back and the return address was a Sydney office. I carefully opened it, trying not to tear the thick paper. Once I pulled out the letter inside, I unfolded it and began reading.

I felt my own eyes widen. An "Oooooh," sound gushed from my lips.

"What is it? What does it say?" KC was leaning forward, trying to read through the paper.

My ears were ringing. I couldn't process the words on the page. I read it through again, but it still didn't compute. "Wow. I wasn't expecting this. I wasn't expecting anything at all."

I turned the letter over and passed it to KC to read for herself. It only took a few seconds. Her mouth popped open. "'Wow' is right!"

I took some deep breaths and decided what I had to do. "I'm calling Deidre for advice."

W hen I finally arrived at work for a midday start, it was all systems go. I worked hard, since the crowds of shoppers were thick now, with only a couple of days to go until Christmas. Even the reluctant older male shoppers were out, looking for easy gift ideas for wives and daughters.

I was preoccupied by the contents of the letter I'd received earlier. All I wanted to do was tell Christos, talk it over with him. But he was nowhere to be seen.

I didn't see Christos for several hours.

In the end I stumbled across him when I took my dinner break. I was working until nine o'clock in the evening and I'd brought my own leftover pizza with me.

He was in the staff break room and he looked half dead, lying on one of the bench seats with his arm thrown over his eyes, as if to block out the light. Shirt untucked and wrinkled, hair tousled, jaw dark with the beginnings of five o'clock shadow. Basically, he was messily gorgeous.

I gently touched his arm, careful not to startle him if he was asleep. "Christos?"

He moved, blinking his eyes and propping himself up to half-sitting. "Lily? I...I must have fallen asleep. Dammit. I need to get going." He tried to stand but as he placed some weight on his right leg, he faltered. He sank onto the seat again.

I sat down beside him. I wanted to climb into his lap and kiss him, but I restrained myself. Barely. "Are you all right? You look wrecked. Handsome, but wrecked."

He glanced around the room. I guessed I wasn't supposed to call him handsome at work, but we were alone. "It's been busy. I worked through the night. We think something's going down tomorrow. I can't say much."

I stared into Christos's eyes for a beat or two. So many questions were on the tip of my tongue, and my news from the letter was burning a hole in my brain. But I couldn't talk about any of it now. I smoothed my hands down my black skirt. I had to do something.

"Let me make you a coffee." I headed over to the laminate bench defining the kitchenette area of the room, grabbing a mug from the overhead cabinets and firing up the mini espresso machine.

He called out across the room. "You don't have to get me anything."

I ignored him. I made the coffee because I wanted to. White with one. A warm glow spread through my chest because I knew how he liked his coffee. I added the spoon of sugar to the cup and stared at it.

Coffee making shouldn't have that effect on me. The glowiness was all because of Christos, and my wanting to please him. I pressed my lips together, because it was blindingly obvious.

I *loved* him. I'd fallen in love with Christos. I hadn't even been trying. I wanted to tell him, right that second. Because as Harry said to Sally, when you realise you want to spend the rest of your life with someone, you want the rest of your life to start as soon as possible.

But what if the revelation, the shock, was too much? It was more than my mind could handle.

I turned to face Christos, who was sitting with his chin in his hands. I couldn't speak. I grabbed the coffee I'd made him and walked like a robot to the other side of the room. I plonked the cup down on the table in front of him.

His expression softened. The look he shot me should have been illegal. My body heated and I wanted to kiss him, and tackle him to the ground. Get rid of all those useless clothes until he was gloriously naked.

Christos seemed to have an inkling of my thoughts. "Thanks, Lily." His voice had deepened, pure passion laced with humour.

"I...I have to go!" I whirled around and headed for the door, forgetting about my pizza and leaving the man I loved sitting there staring at me walking away.

I had a Christmas present to buy. Maybe the most important one of my life.

CHAPTER 14

❄

CHRISTMAS EVE: PART ONE

Christmas Eve should have been merry and bright, preferably white. Instead, I woke to the sun streaming through the gap between my poor-quality cotton curtains, a blazing yellow hinting at more heat. I'd woken up sweating.

I'd been having a delicious and dirty dream. Christos and I were marooned on a Greek island without any clothes. It was just heating up (so to speak) when I blinked my eyes open. *Dreamus interruptus.* When I rolled out of bed, I sweated a little more. Seven in the morning and it was sticky already. And I missed Christos.

I pulled on my kimono, which had been hanging on the back of my bedroom door. I'd slept in only a cotton sheet and a hint of my favourite perfume dabbed on my pulse points.

I checked the weather forecast app on my phone. Horror! The temperature was predicted to hit thirty-nine degrees Celsius. Over a hundred degrees in the 'old money', as my gran would have said.

Urgh. This day would be the death of me. Well, maybe not death, but torture. I looked at the item of clothing hanging on my wardrobe door and grumble-sighed. It was a short dress of sorts, red velvet with long sleeves, trimmed with white fur. Not only was it a horrid design for my shape, but I'd have to suffer the indignity of dressing up as Sexy Santa, or maybe Mrs Claus with missing pants. It would be stifling to wear today.

The fabulous idea was courtesy of our store manager. He wanted everyone on the cosmetics floor dressed in costume for Christmas Eve. To be extra festive.

I couldn't wear it walking down the street though. I'd have to take it with me and change when I got to work. I narrowed my eyes at the offending outfit as I stomped out of the bedroom, down the hall and into the kitchen.

The open plan kitchen/dining area lead through to the living room. As I stood at the counter, I spied KC standing in the corner of the living room. She was dressed in her more usual gear, denim shorts and a floaty red top. She was hanging shiny baubles on the six-foot-tall plastic fir tree in the corner of the room.

I'd had the Christmas tree up for over a week without actually decorating it. I couldn't do it after coming home from work. I was nearly done in, mentally and physically. So it was great to see KC taking on the decorating task. It was homey somehow.

Ignoring my need for coffee, for now, I made my way across the living room to my sister's side. She glanced at me over her shoulder, grinned and continued with her work. Now she was winding an armful of tinsel around the tree in great swathes.

KC waved vaguely around the room. "I thought we needed some Christmas cheer around here." She turned and grabbed my arm. "What are we doing for Christmas Day? Should we have dinner at home? I can go shopping while you're at work."

Oh. I was a horrible person. I hadn't even thought about it. I'd assumed Bill would be around and we'd do something simple, like lunch at the local pub. Now KC was here, I wanted to do something more special.

Picking up a bauble from the box on the floor, I hung it on the tree. "Let's do a nice dinner at home. We don't need a turkey, but maybe seafood, or chicken with salads? And dessert. I think Pavlova is in order."

KC jumped up and down. "Oh, yes. Pav, and those little chocolate ball things Dad used to make. I'll make a list!" She dashed off to grab her phone, tapping out reminders in her shopping-list app.

I picked up a shoebox full of ornaments and whipped off the lid, expecting to see more gaudy baubles like the scarlet and emerald glittery ones on the tree. What I found was something else entirely. A treasure. Mum's ornaments from when we were little—a silver angel figurine and two tiny heart-shaped photo frames holding pictures of both me and KC as babies.

I gulped back a sob as I removed them from the tissue paper inside the box. I placed the angel on the table nearby, and raised the two photos, dangling by the golden threads attached. KC faced me now, her face pale. She reached for her own image and carefully took it from me.

KC's voice cracked as she spoke. "How did they end up here?"

"I suppose Bill got some of Dad's stuff when he…" I didn't say any more. I couldn't. I shut my eyes tight.

My sister hugged me this time, wrapping her arm around my shoulders. "It's going to be a good Christmas. Don't worry."

I nodded against her shoulder, hoping she was right.

Before I could enjoy Christmas Day with KC, I had to get through the rest of Christmas Eve. I arrived at work a touch before eight in the morning, and the store was already open. *Jingle Bell Rock* pumped relentlessly through the store's speakers.

Lost souls wandered through the aisles like someone had opened the gates of hell. Or forgotten to close the gates last night, more likely. The store had been open for the infamous twenty-four-hour, round-the-clock trade. An extremely drunk couple lolloped past me as I crossed the floor heading for the perfume counter. They looked the worse for wear and I'd lay bets they'd been shopping and drinking through the night. Great for the store's profits, not so great for the staff.

"Heads up, Santa's already here!" shouted the woman, pointing at me with a bony finger outstretched. "Nah, it's one of Santa's slutty helpers." She crashed into her boyfriend, slapping his back. They both burst into raucous laughter.

I glanced down at my ridiculous outfit. She was right. The look had veered away from wholesome and verged on Santa's naughty calendar-girl assistant. I sighed and kept walking. At least my favourite scarlet high heels would give me good-looking legs.

I strode to my counter, keeping my head held high in my Santa hat with the little bell, jingling all the way. Three staff were on deck, all exhausted. Giselle leaned one elbow on the counter. She was also wearing her silly costume. The others, Gillian and a casual girl, Davina, with the greenest cat-like eyes (possibly contacts), were stuck wearing the full-body onesies and reindeer antlers. Honestly, I was one of the lucky ones.

"Good morning," I chirped in a sing-song voice. I wanted to inject some positivity into the team, jingling as I moved behind the counter.

Giselle snorted. "It is morning, but I would not say it is good. *C'est la vie.*"

Right. Judging by the bags under the other two women's eyes, the night shift had been trying. "Who needs a break?" All three women stuck their hands in the air. "Um, Giselle, you're due to go home at nine. Grab a coffee and come back in fifteen minutes. Then you ladies can take turns."

Everyone nodded. Giselle slunk away, tearing off her Santa hat from her head as she went.

A rush of customers started and didn't stop until lunchtime. Another casual staff member joined our team, spritzing a perfume we wanted to sell-out before Christmas. Her name was Xanthe. She was short, dark and bouncy from her black curly hair to her sparkly shoes. She was doing a fabulous job being chatty.

"Experience the warm scent of gardenias and lily of the valley." Xanthe beamed and passed out pre-sprayed sample cards to passing customers. "I know you'll love it."

I was busy serving a mature gentleman who was alarmingly orange. I'm not one to make judgements, but I think he'd either eaten too many carrots or swallowed a bunch of self-tanning pills. In any case, I was afraid he was radioactive.

I ducked below the counter to pull two gift sets out of the glass-fronted cabinet. I stood up and placed them in front of him. "This one is lovely. It's a sophisticated Parisian scent with a top note of peony and a base note of lavender. The eau de parfum is the concentrate, so it lasts longer on the skin. It's great value combined with the free gift."

He nodded, then pointed to the other set. "What about this one?"

"It's perhaps suited to a younger woman, because it's a fun, flirty scent with a hint of apple and citrus. The shower gel is a perfect travel size for the holidays too."

I passed him a sample card of each fragrance, since he didn't want me spritzing his skin. Once he'd inhaled them both, he broke into a broad grin. "I'll take them both. One for wifey, one for the girl on the side, if you get my meaning."

"Haha," I laughed in a rather forced way, taking the credit card he thrust towards me and turning away.

Spare me from the philandering older men who thought they were Casanovas. I was constantly amazed they thought I'd find them hilarious.

"Wrap 'em up pretty, would you, sweetheart?"

"Of course, sir."

I wrapped, sticky-taped and be-ribboned like a professional, and completed the transaction with a smile. Because I only had a few more hours until I could go home.

I handed over the merchandise to the orange-faced adulterer and thankfully he left. Before I had a chance to add up the sales figures for the day, restock the cabinet or do anything else, a piercing screech sounded from all directions.

I slapped my hands over my ears as a blast of static ripped through the PA system. I looked around to find most of the staff and customers doing the same. What was going on?

A burst of scarlet and gold caught my attention from the corner of my vision. In the centre of the main aisle, a gigantic gift box had appeared. It was big enough to hold a person.

Sure enough, the lid opened, as if it was being pulled up by an invisible string, and a woman popped her head up from inside. Music blared from the speakers now, a tune I recognised—*You Make Me Feel Like Christmas* by Gwen Stefani. The woman inside the box rose until she was standing on top of a pedestal. She was wearing an exact copy of my outfit. She was dancing, moving like a robot, arms pistoning up and down.

Next came a flurry of movement from the other side of the floor. A whole procession of spritzer chicks, half dressed in the vile onesies, half in sexy Santa dresses, dancing as they walked. The whole thing reminded me of a music video, the proper old-school choreographed ones starring Pat Benatar or Michael Jackson.

Customers jumped back, out of the way, as the chorus line approached. The women were all smiling like robots too. I couldn't see who was in charge. I shot a glance at the security entrance and spotted Christos, standing tall, tense, arms crossed. He didn't appear to know what was happening any more than I did.

Petula was suddenly standing on the other side of my counter. "Hey, what's all this?" She waved her hands around, encompassing the whole shebang.

I shrugged, keeping my eyes on Christos. "I wish I knew. You'd think the management would tell the floor staff about a flash mob."

I knew I should keep out of it, whatever 'it' was, but I gravitated towards Christos with my eyes, my whole body. "Excuse me, I think I'll go check-in with security."

Petula nodded and waved me off. I hotfooted it across the floor, keeping well clear of the main aisle. I rounded the back of the cosmetics area, skirted the evening dresses in women's fashion and approached Christos from his left-hand side as he was talking into his phone. He ended the call and flicked his gaze to me.

One side of Christos's full mouth quirked upwards. "Well, hello. I've never been attracted to Santa's elves before, but I'll make an exception for you."

I held out my tiny skirt and did a curtsy. "Gee, thanks. Did you know about this performance?"

His face went stony again. "Not exactly. But we

were expecting something to happen today." He shifted closer to me, and spoke in a low commanding tone. "I'd suggest you go back to your counter and stay there. Go!"

CHAPTER 15

CHRISTMAS EVE: PART TWO

My mouth was hanging open. I was shocked by Christos's change of tone. When I glanced over his shoulder, I spotted Jason and a few other security staff I didn't recognise coming our way. Christos stared me down, then subtly nodded.

I took off, back the way I'd come, keeping clear of the spritzer chicks who were still dancing in formation. People were clapping and cheering, as one girl led the others in a dance with swooping hand movements and a kind of hip-hop grind.

I clacked across the marble floor in my high heels, rounding the counter and stopping near the cash register as another ear-splitting noise vibrated through the PA system. With my hands pressed firmly to my ears, the same as everyone else, I looked back for

Christos. I couldn't see him or the rest of the security team.

Did Christos think the security team were untrustworthy? It was a possibility. I kept my ears covered even as the sound died down and the song switched to *All I Want for Christmas Is You*. Mariah Carey's voice rang out and the dancers changed to an upbeat routine.

But then... I stopped dead. Let my hands drop to my sides. Now I'd seen it, it was obvious. They were trying to distract people. The gorgeous and gigantic cut-crystal display perfume bottle was gone. Vanished. *Poof!* When had I last seen it? Not that morning, not that I could recall.

An empty white pedestal stood in the area near the escalators. How could anyone take something so enormous without being noticed?

I didn't have to wait long for an answer as I scanned the floor. A team of what appeared to be visual merchandising staff was moving through the fashion department, pulling something on an industrial-sized trolley. The thing was draped in a black cloth. It could have been stock, maybe furniture or fixtures. They needed to get ready for the Boxing Day sale starting in two days. But I knew something was off.

A gang of people, probably not real staff, was absconding with the super-expensive and collectable perfume bottle while everyone was oblivious. And they were headed for the main storeroom.

I couldn't let it go. I had to report it to Christos. He

was the only one who'd know what to do. I took off again, pausing only to wave at a couple of staff who shot me questioning looks. I mimed fanning my face, pretending to be too hot. No one would have a problem with me leaving the floor for a minute for a drink of water.

I kept on the tail of the gang of people dressed in black. Sure enough, one of them scanned a staff card and unlocked the storeroom. The group wheeled the trolley through the double doors and out of view. I stopped and twirled around, checking in all directions, but there was no Christos.

There was nothing else for it. I'd have to follow the sneaky gang. As I approached the storeroom, trying to walk at a normal pace, I spotted two more people clad in black, carrying arm loads of Christmas gifts. The same type of fake presents we'd had on display through the department. They too entered the storeroom with the beep of a staff card. I was a few metres away, nego-tiating my way through racks of suits and shirts.

At the door, I grabbed my staff card and scanned it. I was probably being watched on the security cameras and tracked by my ID. But tracked by who? I hoped it was Christos, but I had my doubts. Who was in charge around here? I clicked open the door, sliding inside.

Everything looked normal at first glance. I took tiny steps, keeping close to the wall separating the store-room from the sales floor. The muffled sound of music was playing through the concrete. This space was like a bunker. Traces of shivers, invisible fingers, ran down my spine. I shouldn't have come in here by myself. If I had to run, my only way out was behind me. I turned to backtrack when a shaft of sunlight fell across the floor.

Someone had opened the garage doors leading out the back of the store. The loading area wasn't accessible to everyone, not even me. But it was open now. I squeezed my eyes shut. I knew I should run, but I couldn't leave.

Blinking my eyes open, I crept past rows of shelving stacked with cosmetics products. Muffled voices came from the direction of the loading bay. It was too hard to hear distinct words but there were several men. I slid off my heels and left them by the wall. My footfalls with bare feet were quieter. I could also run faster if necessary.

Popping my head from behind a metal shelving unit, I got a view of the open garage doors. A truck had backed up there. Several men loaded piles of gift boxes into the back and the gigantic trolley sat to one side.

I sneaked back behind the shelving. My heart thumped so hard I thought I'd break a rib. I pressed one hand to my chest.

A thud from behind me had me spinning round to face the largest man I'd ever seen in my life. I looked up, and up, his tree-trunk of a neck leading to a face defined by a flat nose and shaved head.

He stared me down as though I were something

he'd scrape off the bottom of his shoe. "What have we here?" He grabbed my arm before I respond.

"I'm getting some perfume, heading back to the floor…"

He yanked me towards him. "Like hell you are."

Something silvery glinted in his hand and for a heartbeat I thought it was a gun. Thank goodness it was just handcuffs. Only he snapped one cuff shut around my wrist and my thoughts raced in terrible circles. If he wanted to hurt me, I couldn't get away. A bent Christmas tree with a metal frame had been left in the corner.

The man shoved me to the ground, I thudded onto my bottom, and struggled to get up. But I didn't have any choice once he kneeled on my leg and pulled on my arm, twisting it behind me. The bruising pressure made me gasp, air leaving my body in a gush. The snap of the other cuff set-off full-blown panic inside me. He'd cuffed me to the metal pole of the Christmas tree. I tugged and twisted, trying to get free. All I did was hurt my wrist.

The thug huffed smoke-tinged breath over me. Yuck. "That should hold you for a while. Merry Christmas, Mrs Claus." He raised himself to standing and took off, footsteps echoing as he headed towards the truck outside.

The dull rumble of the truck's engine was the soundtrack in the room now. The scent of exhaust fumes acrid, burning my nostrils. With another tug at the handcuffs, I tried to get loose from the bloody tree, or to break it. It was stronger than it seemed, weighted by a heavy stand. Pulling it along behind me wasn't an option.

I sighed and sank back against the trunk, fake pine needles poking into me. At least the store was still open. Someone had to find me soon. If not Christos, someone.

"Hello?" I shouted into the void for approximately the seventy-thousandth time. There had to be someone around. Anyone? Could they come soon?

I wasn't sure how much time had passed. Of course it seemed endless, since there was nothing to do but stare at the rows of stock on metal shelving, some items in boxes, some loose. In my head, I developed a much-improved storage and cataloguing system I'd implement if I ever got a chance. At this rate, it wasn't likely.

A thunderous crash rang out like a tractor ploughing into a wall. It came from near the door where I'd entered the storeroom. Another bang, then light flooded inside followed by the thud of footsteps. I stayed immobile, waiting for a sign. Was it friend or foe?

"Lily? Are you in here?"

It was Christos, without a doubt.

I sat up straighter. "Here! By the Christmas tree."

He skidded around a corner, then he was there. By my side. He scanned my body quickly, assessing me with a glance. "I'm so sorry I got you dragged into this." Crouching down, he checked my leg, running his palm over my shin. It smarted.

"I'm handcuffed." I rattled my chains, feeling like a convict.

He tipped his head to the side. "Shit. I don't have a key, or tools. Hold tight, I'll be back for you soon."

I gaped at him, as he pressed a kiss to my forehead. He was up and walking away in a split second.

With a rising panic, I begged, "Don't leave me here! If you wanted me handcuffed you only had to ask!"

He snorted as he walked out and the door slammed shut again. So glad he was amused.

Lucky (for Christos) it was only a couple of minutes later when he returned. I'd been planning to do him bodily harm until I spotted the toolbox he carried. When a police officer in uniform followed him into the storeroom, talking on a walkie-talkie, I was doubly relieved.

I kept my eyes on Christos's face. "Does this mean you caught the thieves? I saw them, loading stuff into the truck. Empty gift boxes and the giant perfume bottle." I was rambling, but I didn't care.

Christos searched the toolbox and pulled out a small and lethal-looking pointy thing. He twisted it into the lock on the handcuffs. He nodded as he worked. "It's all over. We got the guys and the truck—

we were waiting for them at the end of the driveway. And those boxes weren't empty. They've been transferring cash out of the upstairs safe into gift boxes for weeks, then they moved the boxes into the storeroom. Just waiting for a pick up on Christmas Eve."

"Wowsers. Organised crime for sure. Who was the ringleader?"

Two more police officers entered the storeroom and Christos glanced over his shoulder. "I can't talk about it yet." He shot me the same look from earlier. Asking me without words to trust him.

He jiggled the tool in the lock and with a final click, I was free.

"Thanks." I wriggled as he rubbed my sore wrist, and not just because my hand had gone numb. When he was near, I couldn't help getting my wiggle on.

He helped me to my feet, brushed my hair back from my shoulders and offered me his arm. "Let's get you home."

We'd made it out of the storeroom/prison when the nearby elevator opened. Two more uniformed cops were 'escorting' a man in handcuffs out of the doors. A man I recognised, though I didn't know him well.

I called out to him. "Mr Harrison?"

He looked up at the sound of his name, and frowned as though trying to work out if he knew me. The cops urged him forward, then he was gone.

I whispered to Christos, who ushered me towards

the staff exit. "The store manager was the ringleader? But his family own the store. Why?"

Christos shrugged. "Would it be too simple to say he fell in with the wrong crowd? He owed them a lot of money and they demanded it back, with interest. And he wanted to impress his lady-friend."

Please don't say Giselle. I'd suspected she liked the store manager. Probably more like she had a massive crush. I had to know. "Who was the woman?"

"Oh, the movie star. Veronica Versuvius. Can't say I like her much. Classic over-actor. She wanted the giant crystal perfume bottle and demanded he get it for her."

My mouth popped open. I couldn't think what to say. The whole adventure was like a Bond movie, one of the good ones from the 80s. The only thing missing was a villain with an eye patch and a tank full of sharks. I decided we'd better go while the going was good.

And I couldn't wait to get my undercover agent home and show him how much I appreciated him.

I whispered, "Will you take me home?"

"Absolutely. Got to make sure you're home in time for Christmas."

EPILOGUE

❄

CHRISTMAS MORNING

The morning dawned. Too early, too bright. I opened one eye a crack and sighed.

There was a hot, handsome man lying beside me. He was taking up too much space in my bed and snoring lightly, but I didn't mind. I suspected this man could even convert me into a morning person.

Christos shifted, rubbing his hand over his face, then he grinned. "Merry Christmas, Lily."

My voice was husky. "Merry Christmas to you."

He leaned over and kissed my lips. It only lasted a few seconds, but it made my heart thud, my blood pump wildly. What a way to wake up, on a day brimming with new beginnings.

Christos raised one eyebrow, while toying with the

edge of the sheet pulled up over my breasts. "Can I ask a dumb question?"

"Uh-huh."

He hesitated. "What have you got planned today? I thought we could do something. Together."

"You mean like an actual date?" It was a good idea. I approved. There was only one catch. "I already said I'd do Christmas dinner with KC."

He shrugged, circling one maddening fingertip round and round the point of my right nipple, covered only by the sheet. "She could come along."

I sat up, my eyes widening with surprise. "I don't know what kind of thing you're into, but a two-for-one special on sister-girlfriends is not on offer."

He shook with laughter, until the whole bed vibrated. Then he rolled to his side and spoke close to my ear. "You're a crack-up. I'm not interested in a two-for-one. But you could both come along to my family's Christmas lunch at my yia-yia's house."

"Your grandmother? Christmas lunch? Meet the whole family?"

He smiled, in the twinkly way I adored. "Yeah, I think you should meet them." He shrugged again, but I wasn't fooled by his casualness. There was something serious in his darkening eyes. "I want to introduce you to my family. I love you, Lily Lucas. They're going to love you too."

Well, if hearts could leap right out of chests, I'd have been scraping mine off the ceiling. Instead, I leapt on

Christos. I straddled his waist, throwing all pretence of covering my nakedness out the proverbial window. "I love you too!" I smooshed down and crushed my body against his.

He groaned, reached for my face and his mouth covered mine in lingering, delicious kiss.

"You smell so good," I whispered against his cheek.

He rolled so I was flat on my back. "I almost forgot. I've got a present for you."

I tried to stop him, but he got up, out of the bed. He grabbed his sports bag sitting on the floor. When he pulled out a beautifully wrapped gift in a tiny little shopping bag, I nearly squealed. He handed it to me without speaking.

I opened the bag and pulled out a golden embossed box. An exquisite, miniature cut-crystal bottle shaped like a heart was inside. I released the old-fashioned stopper and inhaled the heavenly scent within. The fragrance wound around me, the perfect, simple essence of my favourite flower in the whole world.

"It's a concentrate from Paris. Lily of the Valley, for my Lily. The manager of the perfume store said it was the best quality."

"Oh, I love it. It's just like the ones used to blend perfumes in France."

I sat up and gasped, smacking my hand over my mouth. I let it drop to my lap and took Christos's hand. I carefully placed my perfume on the bedside table.

"I didn't get a chance to tell you. I have the most

amazing news." In all the action and mayhem, I'd forgotten about yesterday's letter. "I received a letter from a solicitor. My boss back in Sydney passed away earlier this year. Well, Judith was my mentor, like family. It turns out she left me quite a large sum of money in her will. More than one hundred thousand dollars."

Christos let out a low whistle. "Seriously? Great news. It's not my business, but that's going to help pay for KC's college, right?"

I nodded. It was exactly what I'd been planning. But there was more. "I also want to rent a shop for my own perfumery. I have to find the right place, and consult a lawyer friend, but I think I can do it."

"Of course you can. I'm so happy for you." He kissed me again and this time I pulled him closer.

I broke the kiss only when I remembered I had a present for Christos too. I pressed a finger to his mouth. "Wait a second." Reaching into the drawer of the bedside table, I grabbed the smaller gift box.

I passed it to Christos and waited until he lifted the lid and saw the item enclosed.

He lifted the red satin ribbon, a metallic shape attached. "A key?" His eyebrow arched in question.

"It's a symbol, a key to my heart. Also it's actually a key to this house. Because I want you to feel welcome here, with me."

This time Christos wrapped his strong arms right

around me and pulled me into a bear hug. He was so sweet, tears threatened to spill from my eyes.

"Thank you."

I sighed against his shoulder, kissing the spot at the base of his throat that made him shiver. I pulled away, only for a minute. "One more present."

The larger gift box was navy blue and manly. Which was tricky of me, considering the contents.

I pulled the gift out of the box and held it up in mid-air. The glow-in-the-dark handcuffs with the fluffy pink fur lining were a work of art. "I really do want you to cuff me."

He chuckled against my side, then pressed his lips to the upper swell of my breast. I couldn't breathe for a second. He snatched the cuffs from my hand. "You asked for it."

I did. I asked for it over and over.

What more could a girl ask for? Only many, many more blissful, sweetly scented Christmases with the man I loved.

❄

Before you go... Don't forget to sign-up for my newsletter!
Go to **cassandraolearyauthor.com/contact** for updates on my new writing,
deals and giveaways.

GLOSSARY

AUSSIE SLANG & PHRASES IN HEART NOTE

As an author, I like to use authentic slang and phrases typical of the story setting and to suit voice of my characters.

I'm Australian, and I've used some Aussie language and spelling in this book. These are not mistakes, just differences in local language. You little ripper!

- big ask – a big favour or request
- carpark – parking lot
- crack-up – to laugh, or an amusing person
- divvy van – divisional van or police car, usually from the local police station
- dead-set – for certain
- dobbing – telling tales or reporting someone to authorities
- goodies – treats or sweets

- nong – a fool
- Pavlova/Pav – popular meringue dessert topped with whipped cream and fruit
- shopping centre – an indoor mall
- spunk – a handsome man, worth having a crush on

Have a good one!
  Cassandra x

ACKNOWLEDGMENTS

The inspiration for this story came from the approximately six years I worked as a perfume counter sales assistant/promotions team member/beauty advisor in some of Australia's largest department stores. I relied on that job while I was at university (in two different courses, long story), working part-time during semester and usually full-time over the summer break. Yes, I worked the dreaded 24-hour trading, 23rd December to Christmas Eve shift, my eyes hanging out of my head while incessantly smiling, dressed glamorously in high heels and a pencil skirt. I wrapped more gift sets than I could possibly count. I was yelled at by an old man who wanted a specific gift for his mistress, all while selling him another gift for his wife. I watched some of my less-than-nice colleagues polish their shoes with the expensive face cream samples. You really do get to experience the best and worst of humanity when you work retail!

I'd like to acknowledge the generous support of my readers, especially those who took a chance on my first few indie published works. You are all awesomesauce. I hope you enjoyed reading this novella. If so, please check out my other books and short reads on my website at cassandraolearyauthor.com – and don't forget to sign-up for my newsletter! I do remember to send it out occasionally...

Thanks to my wonderful writing group, the Melbourne Romance Writers Guild, who helped me develop my writing craft, specifically how to write a romance, and with brainstorming mad ideas for this novella. You all rock!

Thanks also to my friends and colleagues in Romance Writers of Australia, who have taught me so much and are just generally switched-on and fabulous. You all inspire me more than you know.

I'm so thankful for the amazing cover design by Lana Pecherczyk (a great writer too) and professional editing by Ruth Kennedy. My excellent author friend PJ Vye worked on the layout for this print edition and talked me into doing a paperback, like an absolute boss babe.

And most of all, thank you to my darling husband, who knew me way back when. You put up with my retail stories back in the day and bought me a foot bath to soak my aching feet at the end of my shifts. Now you support me in my writing ambitions like a genuine hero. Love, always.

ABOUT THE AUTHOR

Cassandra O'Leary is a romance and women's fiction author, freelance writer and communications specialist who escaped a corporate communications career to focus on fiction writing. In 2015, Cassandra won the global We Heart New Talent writing contest run by HarperCollins UK, and her debut novel, *Girl on a Plane*, was released in 2016. This novel was also translated into Czech as *Letuska*. Since then, Cassandra has independently published several novellas and short stories and had stories featured in two romance anthologies. She's working on multiple novels and probably will be, forevermore.

Cassandra is a mother of two gorgeous, high-energy mini ninjas and wife to a spunky superhero. Living in Melbourne, Australia, she's also travelled the world. If you want to send her to Italy or Spain on any food or wine tasting 'research' trips, that would be splendiferous. You'll find her on social media, drinking coffee, reading all the books, cooking gluten free treats and (possibly) buying shoes and beauty products on the internet.

Proud member of Romance Writers of Australia, and the Melbourne Romance Writers Guild.

Follow Cassandra on social media:
    Facebook - facebook.com/cassandraolearyauthor
    Twitter @cass_oleary
    Instagram @cassandissima

Read more at cassandraolearyauthor.com

Lightning Source UK Ltd.
Milton Keynes UK
UKHW041041251121
394585UK00001B/151